PRAYING IN THE PRESENCE OF

OUR LORD

WITH
MOTHER
TERESA

D0354493

SUSAN CONROY

FR. BENEDICT J. GROESCHEL, C.F.R.
SERIES EDITOR

Our Sunday Visitor Publishing Division
Our Sunday Visitor, Inc.
Huntington, Indiana 46750

Nihil Obstat:
Rev. Michael Heintz
Censor Librorum

Imprimatur:
✠ John M. D'Arcy
Bishop of Fort Wayne-South Bend
February 9, 2005

The *nihil obstat* and *imprimatur* are declarations that a work is free from doctrinal or moral error. It is not implied that those who have granted the *nihil obstat* and *imprimatur* agree with the contents, opinions, or statements expressed.

The Scripture citations contained in this work are taken from the *Revised Standard Version of the Bible — Catholic Edition* (RSV), copyright © 1965 and 1966 by the Division of Christian Education of the National Council of the Churches of Christ in the United States of America. Used by permission. All rights reserved.

Every reasonable effort has been made to determine copyright holders of excerpted materials and to secure permissions as needed. If any copyrighted materials have been inadvertently used in this work without proper credit being given in one form or another, please notify Our Sunday Visitor in writing so that future printings of this work may be corrected accordingly.

Our Sunday Visitor Publishing Division
Our Sunday Visitor, Inc.
200 Noll Plaza
Huntington, IN 46750

ISBN: 1-59276-071-6 (Inventory No. T122)
LCCN: 2004118005

Cover design by Tyler Ottinger
Cover art by Robert F. McGovern
Unless otherwise noted, photos provided by author;
all photos used with permission.
Interior design by Sherri L. Hoffman

PRINTED IN THE UNITED STATES OF AMERICA

✠

For Our Savior Jesus —
through the Immaculate Heart of Mary

Contents

✠

Foreword

✠

*E*veryone who has been following our series of *Praying in the Presence of Our Lord* books, especially those who use them for Eucharistic adoration, has been waiting for this book. We have all come to know of Mother Teresa's great devotion to Christ in the Eucharist. Those of us who were privileged to know her personally have witnessed her profound devotion and prayerfulness in the presence of Christ in the Eucharist. Now Susan Conroy has given us an insight which will be useful to all Christians in their life of prayer.

Having known Mother Teresa half my life, I can say that it is her devotion to Christ, especially in the Eucharistic presence, that comes back to memory now. I have seen her with the poor and with the saints, with the hierarchy, clergy, and religious, and I have watched her working with the poorest of the poor, some of whom had no idea who she was. I remember her most clearly, however, in the humble chapels of the Missionaries of Charity houses. These memories are graven deeply in my mind and call me to prayer myself, although I could never pray with the intensity and devotion I saw so often in Mother Teresa.

My very last memory of her is beside the Blessed Sacrament in the chapel of the contemplative Missionaries of Charity in the Bronx. She was going the next day to India, and we all knew that she was not well enough to return. Father Andrew Apostoli, C.F.R., and I were privileged to offer Mass for her that day, and I said to Father Andrew as we were leaving, "I'm sure we will never see her again. She is passing through the doors of heaven already." It was, in fact, eight weeks before her death.

The reason I was convinced I would never see her again was that her whole personality was transformed that day in the presence of the Eucharist. There had always been a seriousness about Mother Teresa — a somberness, an engagement in the present situation but always a certain note that in some way she was not enjoying what was going on. It was only later, when her letters to her spiritual directors were published, that I realized what it was. It was her immense thirst for Christ and the feeling of having been rejected and abandoned by Him, which she did not believe but which she did experience. Those unfamiliar with the spiritual life will not understand this. It is, in fact, a very profound example of what we call the dark night of the soul. Our dear mother lived in that dark night for all the years I knew her. On that day of our last meeting, however, when she was just a few feet from the tabernacle, she was like a person transformed. She was joyous, witty, laughing — in fact, she was filled with joy. As odd as the analogy may seem, I told others that she was like a freshly opened ice-cold bottle of champagne. It doesn't fit Mother Teresa, does it? Yet that is what she was like. I realized somehow that she was already entering the doors of paradise. Some of the mystics mention that this can be true of very saintly people as they approach death.

Read, study, and pray with this book. You will learn a great deal about how close Christ can be to someone in this life and lead them to great holiness. To me, Mother Teresa is not only a great saint of our time but also a prophetess of the Christian era. Like Saints Catherine of Siena and Teresa of Ávila, she can be compared with the Old Testament prophetesses. Let us pay her a great compliment by learning from her life, writings, and prayers.

FR. BENEDICT J. GROESCHEL, C.F.R.

Introduction

✠

$\mathcal{M}$other Teresa "longed" for God. Like many of the saints, she longed to belong entirely to God and to love Him "as He has never been loved before." She also wanted Him to be loved by many other souls as well — personally, tenderly, and faithfully.

While we were together at the Motherhouse in Calcutta in 1986, Mother Teresa gave me an old, tattered copy of the *Missionaries of Charity Prayer Book*. Inside the front cover, she added a personal touch, a hand-written note: "Be only all for Jesus through Mary. God bless you. M. Teresa, M.C."

Ten years later, Mother Teresa gave me permission to share her words and teachings in the form of a book — "for the glory of God and for the good of souls." She encouraged me to "do it with Jesus and for Jesus." More

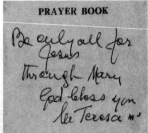

recently, while receiving the blessing of her successor, Sister Nirmala, and gathering material for this new book, I sensed that Blessed Mother Teresa of Calcutta has been "smiling" on this endeavor to help us pray in the presence of Our Lord. Every time I see a sign of Mother's own nod of approval from heaven, my heart is filled with a renewed sense of joy and thanksgiving.

I am so happy to share Mother Teresa and her spirituality with the world. I consider Mother to be one of the greatest saints of all times — a gift from God to us all — in the same way that the life of Saint Francis of Assisi is a timeless gift. I hope that sharing the prayers and inspirations which nourished Mother Teresa's interior life can help us to advance on our own spiritual journey to perfect union with God.

The first part of this book contains some of Mother Teresa's favorite inspirational sayings, sprinkled with quotations by other saints. The second part of this book is filled with beautiful prayers and meditations which Mother Teresa herself used to pray. As one friend exclaimed: "If they were good enough for Mother Teresa, they are a hundred times better and more necessary for me!" I want to thank the Missionaries of Charity — especially Sister Nirmala, Sister Priscilla, Father Brian Kolodiejchuk, and Mother Teresa herself — for graciously allowing me to share these

Photo by Paul Hulewicz

I met Mother Teresa's successor, Sister Nirmala, in Rome just weeks after Mother was called home to God in 1997.

precious treasures. May Mother's prayers and words help us grow in grace and holiness alongside the Missionaries of Charity each day, and fulfill Mother Teresa's desire that God be loved more ardently by all of our hearts.

Mother Teresa wanted to give *saints* to the Church — to draw people closer to God and to draw God closer to us. May these pages help to do that in a beautiful way.

You will see that one or two of the prayers speak about the "evangelical counsels" of Poverty, Chastity, Obedience, and Charity. I have left these holy virtues in the prayers, rather than editing them out, because I believe that even we who are living "in the world" are called to practice these virtues which Our Lord Jesus chose to exemplify during His life on earth. These Gospel values are not just for those living in religious communities, but for all who wish to live in imitation of Christ. Poverty, Chastity, Obedience, and Charity are indeed counter-cultural practices in our times, but they absolutely help us to give ourselves "to all those paths and ways the gentle Jesus kept to, as well as all the saints who follow Him" (St. Catherine of Siena).

Let us pray.

☩

*"I pray that this sculpture will help people
to draw closer to God."*

— MOTHER TERESA, MARCH 24, 1997
(the same year Mother Teresa was called home to heaven)

+L.D.M.

MISSIONARIES of CHARITY
54 A, A.J.C. BOSE ROAD
CALCUTTA 700016 INDIA
7th May, 1997

Dear Anne Spillane Moher,

Thank you for the photographs of the
Sculpture you made.
My prayer for you is that, as you
perform this beautiful works of art,
you may allow Jesus — the greatest
sculptor — to mould you into His
image, more each day.
Let us pray.

GOD BLESS YOU.

M. Teresa mc

 Photo by Anne Spillane Moher

This beautiful sculpture of Mother Teresa is displayed in
Saint Joseph Church, 150 Central Avenue, in Dover,
New Hampshire.

PART

I

Lessons from
Mother Teresa

Prayer

☩

"A good person is a prayer."

— ST. CATHERINE OF SIENA

© 1997 Marie Constantin

Photo by Marie Constantin

"Love to pray.
For prayer gives
a clean heart.
And a clean heart
can see God."

Mother Teresa

*M*other Teresa would spend hours each day in the presence of Our Lord in the chapel — and then she would go forth to radiate His love and His presence on the world of our souls. She was like a living prayer.

Mother would remind everyone to "pray the work" — to let everything we do be imbued with the spirit of love and prayer. Turn the ordinary things of everyday life into an opportunity to offer something beautiful to God. Even when Mother Teresa was sitting at her desk signing letters, it was like praying, she said. "When I am writing 'God bless you,' I am praying."

Mother's namesake, Saint Thérèse of Lisieux, said that prayer is simply lifting our mind and heart to God, Who is in everything and Who is within us. The saints teach us to be more mindful of our good God and Our Blessed Mother Mary throughout the day — to invite them into our daily experiences, praise them, call upon them, even when there is no urgent need. Even Our Blessed Mother Mary, the Mother of God, had to scrape the burnt noodles off the bottom of the pan. She had to do the most mundane things, yet she is the most blessed among women. Those simple things of every day life can help us to become holy when we offer them to God with love — when we do everything "with Jesus and for Jesus."

It is clear that Mother Teresa's heart, like the Immaculate Heart of Mary, was with God throughout the day — "habitually with God," as she would say. We could see it in her face, we knew it by her words, and we could certainly feel it in her presence. It was a blessing just to be near her.

Everyone knows that Mother Teresa accomplished such great things and touched literally millions of lives throughout the world. Many people want to know how she was able to do all of this. What is her secret? How was all of this possible in the life of one small person? Mother Teresa herself said: "My secret is quite simple: I pray." Through simple prayer, she had constant access to Almighty God — the very source of all life, holiness, power, and love. And so do we. In Mother Teresa's own words, God's grace, light, and love are "a fruit always in season and within reach of every hand" — and "no limit is set" on how much we may gather by means of prayer. Mother Teresa's blessed life, like the lives of all the saints, is a testimony to this simple truth about the inexhaustibility and accessibility of God's grace, light, and strength to those who pray.

The great Saint Teresa of Ávila once said: "Give me a person who has fifteen minutes of mental prayer daily, and I will give you a saint." The "little" Saint Thérèse of Lisieux, centuries later, wrote: "For me, prayer is an upward leap of the heart, an untroubled glance toward heaven, a cry of gratitude and love which I utter from the depths of sorrow as well as from the heights of joy."

The saints would agree with these encouraging words by Mahatma Gandhi: "It is better in prayer to have a heart without words, than words without a heart." Love is the key. Even Our Lord Himself told us that we did not need to multiply our words when we pray: "Your Father knows what you need before you ask him" (Matthew 6:8).

Let us turn to Mother Teresa's own words about the beauty, purpose, and power of prayer:

"The most important thing is to pray and pray and pray."

"Everything starts from prayer. Without asking God for love, we cannot possess love, and still less are we able to give it to others."

"We need prayer to understand God's love for us."

"Let us improve our spirit of prayer and recollection. Let us free our minds from all that is not Jesus. If you find it difficult to pray, ask Him again and again: 'Jesus, come into my heart, pray with me, pray in me — that I may learn from Thee how to pray.' "[1]

"Love to pray — feel often during the day the need for prayer and take the trouble to pray. Prayer enlarges the heart until it is capable of containing God's gift of Himself. Ask and seek, and your heart will grow big enough to receive Him and keep Him as your own."

"The more you pray, the more you will love to pray — and the more you love to pray, the more you will pray!"

"Prayer is nothing but that oneness with Christ."

"When we have nothing to give — let us give Him that nothingness. When we cannot pray — let us give that inability to Him…. Let us ask Him to pray in us, for no one knows the Father better than He. No one can pray better than Jesus."

The fruit of SILENCE is Prayer
The fruit of PRAYER is Faith
The fruit of FAITH is Love
The fruit of LOVE is Service
The fruit of SERVICE is Peace

Mother Teresa

God bless you
Me Teresa mc

"If we really want to pray, we must first learn to listen, for God speaks in the silence of the heart."

"Souls of prayer are souls of great silence."

"God is the friend of silence. We need to find God, but we cannot find Him in noise, in excitement. See how nature, the trees, the flowers, the grass grow in deep silence. See how the stars, the moon, and the sun move in silence. The more we receive in our silent prayer, the more we can give in our active life. Silence gives us a new way of looking at everything. We need silence in order to touch souls. The important thing is not what we say, but what God says to us, and what He says through us. There is no life of prayer without silence."[2]

"Silence your heart and mind of all useless desires and distractions, so you may be able to listen to Him in the silence of your heart. You will then know for certain what God wants of you."

"Even God Himself cannot fill what is already full."

"Make time for God in your daily life — to be still and know He is God. I am sure you love Him."

"Prayer, to be fruitful, must come from the heart and must be able to touch the heart of God. See how Jesus taught His disciples to pray. Call God your Father, praise and glorify His name. Do His will, ask for daily bread, spiritual and temporal. Ask for forgiveness of your own sins and that we may forgive others — and also for the grace to be delivered from evil which is in us and around us.... Perfect prayer does not consist in many words, but in the fervor of the desire."[3]

"You should always be praying with all your heart and soul."

✠

The following is excerpted from a talk on prayer by Mother Teresa in Berlin, on June 8, 1980:

My secret is quite simple. I pray.

It was the apostles who asked Jesus: "Jesus, teach us how to pray," because they saw Him so often pray and they knew that He was talking to His Father. What those hours of prayer must have been we know only from that continual love of Jesus for His Father, "My Father!" And He taught His disciples a very simple way of talking to God Himself.

Before Jesus came, God was great in His majesty, great in His creation. And then when Jesus came, He became one of us, because His Father and He wanted us to learn to pray by loving one another as the Father has loved Him.

"I love you," He kept on saying; "as the Father loved you; love Him." And His love was the Cross, His love was the Bread of Life. And He wants us to pray with a clean heart, with a simple heart, with a humble heart. "Unless you become little children, you cannot learn to pray, you cannot enter heaven, you cannot see God." To become a little child means to be one with the Father, to love the Father, to be at peace with the Father, our Father.

Prayer is nothing but being in the family, being one with the Father in the Son and the Holy Spirit. The love of the Father for His Son and the Holy

Spirit. And the love, our love for the Father, through Jesus, His Son, filled with the Holy Spirit, is our union with God, and the fruit of that union with God, the fruit of that prayer — what we call prayer. We have given it that name but actually prayer is nothing but that oneness with Christ.

As Saint Paul has said: "I live no longer I, but Christ lives in me." Christ prays in me, Christ works in me, Christ thinks in me, Christ looks through my eyes, Christ speaks through my words, Christ works with my hands, Christ walks with my feet, Christ loves with my heart. As Saint Paul's prayer was: "I belong to Christ and nothing will separate me from the love of Christ." It was that oneness: oneness with God, oneness with the Master in the Holy Spirit.

And if we really want to pray, we must first learn to listen, for in the silence of the heart God speaks. And to be able to hear that silence, to be able to hear God, we need a clean heart; for a clean heart can see God, can hear God, can listen to God; and then only from the fullness of our heart can we speak to God. But we cannot speak unless we have listened, unless we have made that connection with God in the silence of our heart.

And so prayer is not meant to be a torture, not meant to make us feel uneasy, is not meant to trouble us. It is something to look forward to, to talk to my Father, to talk to Jesus, the One to whom I belong: body, soul, mind, heart.

And when times come when we can't pray, it is very simple: if Jesus is in my heart, let Him pray, let me allow Him to pray in me, to talk to His Father in the silence of my heart. Since I cannot speak, He will speak; since I cannot pray, He will pray. That's why often we should say, "Jesus in my heart, I believe in your faithful love for me, I love You." And often we should be in that unity with Him and allow Him, and when we have nothing to give — let us give Him that nothingness. When we cannot pray — let us give that inability to Him. There is one more reason to let Him pray in us to the Father. Let us ask Him to pray in us, for no one knows the Father better than He. No one can pray better than Jesus. And if my heart is pure, if in my heart Jesus is alive, if my heart is a tabernacle of the living God to sanctify in grace: Jesus and I are one. He prays in me, He thinks in me, He works with me and through me, He uses my tongue to speak, He uses my brain to think, He uses my hands to touch Him in the broken body.

And for us who have the precious gift of Holy Communion every day, that contact with Christ is our prayer; the love for Christ, that joy in His presence, that surrender to His love is our prayer. For prayer is nothing but that complete surrender, complete oneness with Christ.

And this is what makes us contemplatives in the heart of the world; for we are twenty-four hours then in His presence: in the hungry, in the naked, in the homeless, in the unwanted, unloved, uncared for — for Jesus said: "Whatever you do to the least of My brethren, you did it to Me" [see Matthew 25:31-46].

Love

"The language God best hears is silent love."

— ST. JOHN OF THE CROSS

Photo courtesy of Missionaries of Charity

*E*verything depends on how we love each other," Mother Teresa said. It is as simple as that.

One afternoon in the Home for the Dying in Calcutta, a man died in my arms. Like an angel of mercy, Mother Teresa came to help me close his eyes and take care of his body. I was sitting on a little stool beside this man's bed, and this was the first time Mother was actually taller than I was. She was standing at my side, looking down at me as I sat there with tears streaming down my face, still holding this man. I will never forget those moments. Mother seemed so touched by the fact that my heart was moved to tears. She looked deep into my eyes and said: "You have received many graces for this."

Later, a tourist came into the Home for the Dying while I was feeding another one of the dying men. She looked down at me as I sat at his bedside and asked quite candidly: "What are your qualifications for doing this?" I think she was expecting to hear a whole litany of training courses and certifications. Instead, I looked up with a big smile and said one word: "Love!"

There are times in life when having simply "hands to serve and a heart to love" can make a world of difference in the lives of others. Mother Teresa also wanted us to have "a joyful willingness to do the most humble work for the sick and dying."

When I first went to India as a 21-year-old to offer my hands and heart to care for the orphans and the destitute, it was a great "eureka" in my life. On that very first day in particular, as I began to minister to the suffering men and women in the Home for the Dying — carefully feeding them one by one, cleaning their beds, holding their hands — I felt such tremendous joy in discovering "I can do it!" Oftentimes we do not realize what we are capable of giving until we reach out and try. I also learned that love is a universal language. It is understood everywhere we go — even in foreign lands. Even though I did not speak the native languages of Hindi or Bengali, I was able to express everything I wished to say to those who were suffering. When I was holding an orphaned child who had been crying, she knew that I loved her. When I was feeding a dying man, he knew that I cared. I didn't need any words. I am convinced that each one of us has so much love to give — especially our young people. We have so much to say with our hearts, our hands, and our energy. We have more than we realize. "When you pray, you must move your feet" (a Hindu expression).

Sprinkled throughout the following chapters are words from the saints. I pay special attention to them because they speak with greatest authority. They have *lived* what they teach — about love, holiness, an intense spiritual life, courage, greatness of heart, etc. — so their words carry much power and influence.

Love is at the heart of holiness. Love is what life is all about. As Mother Teresa used to remind us so memorably: "At the end of our lives, we will not be judged on what kind of car we drove, how much money we made, or how many degrees we earned. At the end of our lives, we will be judged on love — on how well we put our love into living action."

"Beloved, let us love one another; for love is of God, and he who loves is born of God and knows God. He who does not love does not know God; for God is love" (1 John 4:7-8).

Let us now turn to "the woman who loved the world" — the woman whose heart was big enough to love us all. Let us turn to Blessed Mother Teresa's own words about love:

"Love cannot remain by itself — it has no meaning. Love has to be put into action and that action is service.... Our work is only the expression of the love we have for God. We have to pour our love onto someone, and the people are the means of expressing our love for God."

"I have always been too busy to think what America would be like, but what I've seen I'll never forget ... only affection, kindness, and love."

— Mother Teresa's words after her first visit
to the United States in 1960.[4]

"Love proves itself a thousand times a day."

"Each sigh, each look, each act of mine
shall be an act of Love Divine.
And every thing that I shall do
shall be, dear Lord, for love of You."

— from the Missionaries of Charity prayer
"On the Way to the Chapel"

"Do not imagine that love to be true must be extraordinary. No, what we need in our love is the continuity to love the one we love. See how a lamp burns, by the continual consumption of the little drops of oil. If there are no more of these drops in the lamp, there will be no light.... What are these drops of oil in our lamps? They are the little things of everyday life: fidelity, punctuality, little words of kindness, just a little thought for others; those little acts of silence, of look, and of thought, of word, and of deed. These are the very drops of love that make our life burn with so much light."[5]

"It is easy to love people far away. It is not always easy to love those close to us. It is easier to give a cup of rice to relieve hunger than to relieve the loneliness and pain of someone unloved in our own home. Bring love into your home, for this is where our love for each other must start."

"Love begins at home."

> "Pure love is capable of great deeds, and it is not broken by difficulty or adversity. As it remains strong in the midst of great difficulties, so too it perseveres in the toilsome and drab life each day. It knows that only one thing is needed to please God: to do even the smallest things out of great love – love, and always love."
> — St. Faustina Kowalska

"Start by making your own homes places where peace, happiness, and love abound, through your love for each member of your family and for your neighbors."

"Family first."

> "The smallest act of pure love is of more value in God's eyes ... than all other works together."
> — St. John of the Cross

"How can we love God whom we do not see, if we do not love our neighbors whom we see, whom we touch, with whom we live?"

"If we really want to love, we must learn how to forgive before anything else."

"Intense love does not measure, it just gives."

"Give until it hurts — with a smile."

> "Let us love, since that is all our hearts were made for."
> — ST. THÉRÈSE OF LISIEUX

"Be kind and merciful. Let no one ever come to you without leaving better and happier."

"Be the living expression of God's kindness — kindness in your face, kindness in your eyes, kindness in your smile, kindness in your warm greeting."

"God does not look for big things — He looks for how much love we put in the giving."

"We can do no great things — only small things with great love."

"Open your heart to the love of God which He will give you — not to keep, but to share."

"If we pray, we will believe; if we believe, we will love; if we love, we will serve."

"The world today is hungry not only for bread, but hungry for love; hungry to be wanted, to be loved."

> "Beg Our Lord to grant you perfect love. ... He will give you more than you know how to desire."
> — ST. TERESA OF ÁVILA

"You can find Calcutta all over the world if you have eyes to see — wherever there are people who are not loved, not wanted,

not cared for, the rejected and the forgotten. This is the greatest poverty."

"Just begin one at a time. One, one, one. If I had not picked up that first person dying on the street, I would not have picked up the thousands of others later on."

"Let God use you without consulting you."

"We are precious to Him. That man dying in the street — precious to Him. That millionaire — precious to Him. That sinner — precious to Him. Because He loves us."[6]

"God is love — and He loves us. He loves us tenderly. We are precious to Him."

> "The fire of love is more sanctifying that the fire of purgatory."
>
> — ST. THÉRÈSE OF LISIEUX

"A Christian is a tabernacle of the living God. He created me, He chose me, He came to dwell in me, because He wanted me. Now that you know how much God is in love with you, it is but natural that you spend the rest of your life radiating that love."

"Be true co-workers of Christ. Radiate and live His life. Be an angel of comfort to the sick, a friend to the little ones, and love each other as God loves each one of you with a special, most intense love. Be kind to each other in your homes. Be kind to those who surround you. I prefer that you make mistakes in kindness rather than work miracles in unkindness."

> "Nothing is sweeter than love; nothing higher, nothing stronger, nothing larger, nothing more joyful, nothing better, in heaven or on earth."
>
> — ST. THOMAS À KEMPIS

"Will you do something beautiful for God?"

"Love others as God loves you."

✠

Mother Teresa's words from *Such a Vision of the Street*, by Eileen Egan:

> "It is but natural that a deep desire grows in my heart to be with you wherever you are — to love, help, and guide you to become saints."

> "You cannot give what you do not live."

> "Am I convinced of Christ's love for me and mine for Him? This conviction is like a sunlight which makes the sap of life rise and the buds of sanctity bloom. This conviction is the rock on which sanctity is built."

> "Today, as before, when Jesus comes amongst His own, His own don't know Him. He comes in the rotting bodies of the poor. He comes even in the rich who are being suffocated by their riches, in the loneliness of their hearts, and there is no one to

love them. Jesus comes to you and to me. And often, very often, we pass Him by. Here and in many other places such as Calcutta, we find lonely people who are known only by their addresses, by the number of their room. Where are we, then? Do we really know that there are such people? ... These are the people we must know. This is Jesus yesterday and today and tomorrow, and you and I must know who they are. That knowledge will lead us to love them. And that love, to service. Let us not be satisfied with just paying money. Money is not enough. Money can be got. They need your hands to serve them. They need your hearts to love them.... They are there for the finding.... It is written in the Scriptures: 'I looked for one to care for me and I could not find him.' How terrible it would be if Jesus had to say that to us today, after dying for us on the cross."

"We give the dying tender love and care — everything possible that the rich get for their money, we give them for the love of God. If the people in the United States do not answer the needs of other people ... they will miss the touch of Christ in their lives. What is given them is given to share, not to keep."

"At the hour of death, I believe we will be judged according to the words of Jesus, Who has said:

'I was hungry, you gave Me food;
I was thirsty, you gave Me drink;
I was homeless, you took Me in;
I was naked, you clothed Me;
I was sick, you took care of Me;
I was in prison, you visited Me.
Truly I say to you, for as long as you did it to those the least of My brothers, you did it to Me' [see Matthew 25:31-46].

"Gandhi has also said: 'He who serves the poor, serves God.'

"I spend hours and hours in serving the sick and the dying, the unwanted, the unloved, the lepers, the mental — because I love God and I believe His word: 'You did it to Me.' This is the only reason and the joy of my life: to love and serve Him in the distressing disguise of the poor, the unwanted, the hungry, the thirsty, the naked, the homeless — and naturally, in doing so, I proclaim His love and compassion for each one of my suffering brothers and sisters."

Suffering

✠

"It is suffering that draws us nearer to God."

— ST. THÉRÈSE OF LISIEUX

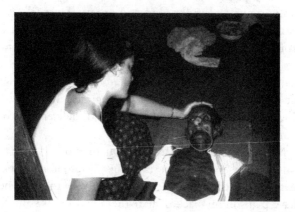

I was taught that suffering excavates a deep place in our souls which can then be filled with God's peace and joy. Mother Teresa would remind us so beautifully that "even Almighty God cannot fill what is already full." So, let us allow this hollowing out in our souls. And know that, even if we are experiencing trials and feelings of emptiness at the moment, we are in prime condition for being filled up with God's inestimable treasures of grace — not the least of which is His own divine presence in our soul.

Mother Teresa truly believed that "suffering is a gift of God," and the Cross is "a place of grace."

In sacred Scripture, we learn that "the LORD reproves him whom he loves, as a father the son in whom he delights" (Proverbs 3:12). Thus, you should "count it all joy … when you meet various trials" (James 1:2). The saints had such intense experiences of suffering — even to the point of shedding blood — and yet they have such beautiful and inspiring things to say about suffering, particularly suffering out of *love* for God and others. They tell us so many hope-filled messages — and their words are like balm to our own aches and wounds. They encourage us to practice patient endurance during our own trials and to see even beauty and value in our afflictions. Seeing the bright side of suffering helps us to get through it: "Many are the afflictions of the righteous; but the LORD delivers him out of them all" (Psalm 34:19).

Mother Teresa shared how a dying man confided in her about how he bore his own sufferings: "Mother, when I get a headache, I share it with Jesus crowned with thorns; when I have pains in my back, I share them with Jesus scourged at the pillar; when my hands and feet hurt, I share it with Jesus nailed to the Cross."[7]

If we desire to live that love which the saints lived — a life in which "each sigh, each look, each act of mine shall be an act of Love Divine" — then we have to live the suffering too. If we want to be true imitators of Christ, then we have to also endure the trials and times of deep loneliness too. It is a package deal. The saints knew all too well that the path of holiness is not all joy and sweetness; it involves periods of misery too. Let us repeat what Saint Thérèse of Lisieux said: "I choose *all*!" My God, I choose all that You will for my life. "It is precisely this attitude of trusting abandonment that elicits divine intervention" (Pope John Paul II).

Here are Mother Teresa's words to inspire us as we carry our own crosses with love:

"My God, give me courage now, this moment, to persevere in doing Your will."

"Very often, small misunderstandings — repeated over and over — become the cause of so much suffering. Bring love to all you do and you will fulfill your vocation."

"This is the time to love like Jesus, with the strength of Jesus. Jesus knew the pain of being rejected by those He loved best and had chosen. But it was for these very same people that Jesus shed His Precious Blood. Ask the Sacred Heart of Jesus to fill you with Jesus' own love ... so that forgiveness may bring peace."

"Either God will shield you from suffering, or God will give you unfailing strength to bear it."
— St. Francis de Sales

"Be like Our Lady who stood near the Cross of Her suffering Son, all the while believing that the resurrection would come. Jesus has promised to answer the persevering prayer of faith."

"Obedience makes us most like Jesus and one with Him. If we really obey, it is a constant crucifixion."

"Remember that the Passion of Christ ends always in the joy of the Resurrection of Christ, so when you feel in your own heart the suffering of Christ, remember the resurrection has to come, the joy of Easter has to dawn. Never let anything so fill you with sorrow as to make you forget the joy of the risen Christ."

> "All who bear their crosses with patience eloquently proclaim Jesus Christ."
>
> — ST. ALPHONSUS LIGUORI

"I am longing with a painful longing to be all for God, to be holy in such a way that Jesus can live His life to the full in me. The more I want Him, the less I am wanted. I want to love Him as He has not been loved — and yet there is that separation, that terrible emptiness, that feeling of absence of God."[8]

"One of the greatest diseases in the world today is to be a nobody to anyone."

"We should not rest in useless looks at our own miseries, but should lift our hearts to God and His light."

> "Sorrow both cleanses the soul and makes peace with God."
>
> — ST. THOMAS À KEMPIS

"I don't think there is anyone else who needs God's help and grace more than I do. I feel so forsaken and confused at times! And I think that's exactly why God uses me: because I cannot

claim any credit for what gets done. On the contrary, I need God's help twenty-four hours a day. And if days were longer, I would need even more of it."[9]

"Alone we can do nothing — but together we can do something beautiful for God."

"Being together is our strength."

"To all who suffer and are lonely, give always a happy smile."

"Suffering, if it is accepted together, borne together, is joy."

"Suffering out of love of God is better than working miracles."

— ST. JOHN OF THE CROSS

Joy

✠

"Every human heart is made for joy."

— POPE JOHN PAUL II

Photo courtesy of CNS

Like love, joy is one of the precious fruits of the Holy Spirit, and it is likewise at the heart of Christianity. Joy is a sign of the hope we have in Our Lord's love and power. As followers of Christ, we have good reason to keep smiling! Saint Ignatius of Loyola encouraged people to "laugh and grow strong," while Saint Francis of Assisi taught: "Do you want to know one of the best ways to win [souls] and lead them to God? It consists in giving them joy and making them happy."

Saint Francis also pointed out that "spiritual joy arises from purity of the heart and perseverance in prayer." Those words could have come from Mother Teresa's own mouth. She often spoke about having a clean heart and praying unceasingly. Mother would add one more ingredient to the recipe for joy, however; and that is *love*. "A joyful heart is the inevitable result of a heart burning with love," Mother used to say. "Love in action *is* joy."

Mother Teresa also taught that when it comes to loving and serving others, joy is half the gift we bring. She reminded us that we are trying to make those who are suffering feel that they are loved, but "if we went to them with a sad face, we would only make them much more depressed."

Mother also pointed to the saints to teach us about the importance of joy: "Saint Francis de Sales said: 'A sad saint is a bad saint.' Saint Teresa of Ávila worried about her sisters only when she saw them lose their joy. Joy is a source of power for us." [10]

Here are more of Mother's beautiful words on joy:

"Joy is prayer. Joy is strength. Joy is love — joy is a net of love by which you can catch souls. She gives most who gives with joy. The best way to show our gratitude to God and the people is to accept everything with joy. A joyful heart is the inevitable result of a heart burning with love."

"We all long for heaven where God is, but we have it in our power to be in heaven with Him right now — to be happy with Him at this very moment. But being happy with Him now means:

> *loving as He loves,*
> *helping as He helps,*
> *giving as He gives,*
> *serving as He serves,*
> *rescuing as He rescues,*
> *being with Him for all the twenty-four hours,*
> *and touching Him in His distressing disguise."*

"Keep the joy of loving Jesus always in your heart — and share this joy with all you meet, and so become an instrument of peace."

"Let us meet God with a smile — everywhere we go and in everyone."

"Joy is very infectious. We will never know just how much good a simple smile can do. Be faithful in little things. Smile at one another. We must live beautifully."

"Be happy and make it a special point to become God's sign of happiness in your community.... Do not tell people of the hard life — just be happy with Christ."[11]

"Today, talking about the poor is in fashion. Knowing, loving, and serving the poor is quite another matter. The little Saint Thérèse said: 'in the heart of the Church, I will be love.' That is what we are — love in the heart of the Church. The password of the early Christians was joy. Serve the Lord with joy."[12]

"You have been given much. Now it is time to share your gifts."

"Joy comes to those who in a sense forget themselves and become totally aware of the other."

"Be the sunshine of God's Love everywhere you go."

"Smile five times a day at someone you don't really want to smile at — do it for peace."

"Let us always meet each other with a smile ... for a smile is the beginning of love."

"I am so used to seeing the smile on our people, even the dying ones smile."

Humility

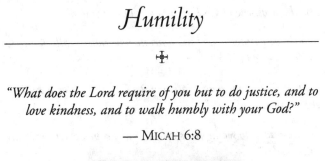

✠

"What does the Lord require of you but to do justice, and to love kindness, and to walk humbly with your God?"

— MICAH 6:8

Photo courtesy of *L'Osservatore Romano*

𝒯rue humility is like a rare pearl. I was completely amazed by the deep humility I witnessed in Mother Teresa of Calcutta. It was as if I had never seen humility before. Being genuinely humble is counter-cultural in this day and age, especially in the West, and yet it is foundational to all other virtues. It is like the solid ground on which everything truly holy is built. In the words of Saint John Vianney: "Humility is to the various virtues what the chain is to the Rosary.

Take away the chain and the beads are scattered; remove humility and all virtues vanish."

God loves the humble heart. Our Lord Jesus repeatedly urged us to humble ourselves, even as He did, and take the form of slaves or servants who are here on earth to love Our Heavenly Father by loving one another. "Learn from me," Our Savior said, "for I am gentle and lowly in heart" (Matthew 11:29).

Mother Teresa felt unworthy of the call that she received from God. She even felt frightened to follow it. But in the end, she surrendered to His will with loving trust, because ultimately her purpose and deepest longing was to be "only all for Jesus" and to please God through perfect obedience to His holy will. She had promised to refuse Him nothing that He might ask — and she stayed true to her promise. She wanted to love Our Lord as He had never been loved before — and love of God always goes hand-in-hand with obedience to His commands.

Mother Teresa was personally called by Our Lord to take care of the poor, the little ones, the dying. She was called to be unafraid and take this leap of faith into the unknown. She was called to carry the light of Christ into the black holes of the slums — because Our Lord wanted to go to the poor, and He wanted the poor to come to Him. From the beginning, He has always loved the lowly ones.

Mother Teresa overcame her initial fears and she trusted in Him. She left the Loretto convent where she had been so happy and so secure — and gave Jesus permission to live His Life "to the full" in her. This dramatically changed the course of her life — and ultimately touched the lives of millions of people throughout the world. She demonstrated love greater than fear. Even decades later, Mother Teresa would be teaching by word and by example: "The good God wants only our love and our trust in Him." With her whole heart, she gave God everything He wanted, and left us a shining example of true holiness and humility.

"The only means of making rapid progress on the way of love is to remain always very *little*" (St. Thérèse of Lisieux). From humility come so many other virtues, because, as Mother Teresa always reminded us, God can easily fill what is empty and humble.

Let us turn to Mother Teresa's own words:

"Let us keep very small."

"If you are humble, nothing will touch you, neither praise nor disgrace, because you know what you are."

"Do not allow yourself to be disheartened by any failure as long as you have done your best."

"He wants us to pray with a clean heart, with a simple heart, with a humble heart."

"Pray lovingly like children, with an earnest desire to love much."

"How great is the humility of God to use people like you and me to bring His love and compassion to those who are suffering. Let us thank God for allowing us to be channels of His love."

"I am nothing. He is everything. I do nothing on my own. He does it. That is what I am: God's pencil.... However imperfect instruments we may be, He writes beautifully."

I will always remember a gentle, handsome, bearded young man in the Home for the Dying in Calcutta. He was one of the patients brought in from the streets. He would sit on his bed with his knees close to his chest and he would quietly watch as I served the other dying men. He seemed very shy. From time to time, I would look over at him, while I was feeding another patient. The minute he saw me glance over, his eyes would turn downward towards his bed. Since he could actually sit up in his bed, I thought he was all right compared to the other patients who had no strength left at all. Because of his appearance, I didn't realize how serious his condition was. I used to concentrate on the ones I thought were most critical and most near death.

One afternoon, I noticed that this young man was on the floor and apparently in great pain. I stayed with him that entire afternoon, getting him cool water, rubbing his back and just being with him in his agony. He died that very night. I didn't even know he was so mortally ill. He had been so patient and gentle as he waited. He never called out for any attention or care. He just waited patiently until his suffering brought him to the floor at the very end.

I still remember his handsome face, and especially his quiet nature. "The poor are great people," Mother Teresa used to say; "they can teach us many beautiful things." I would pray with all my heart to become more like these dying men who were poor in spirit because they were so holy and humble, like the saints.

— SUSAN CONROY

"I am so small, so empty, so nothing — only Jesus can stoop so low as to use one such as me." [13]

"God has shown His greatness by using nothingness — so let us always remain in our nothingness, so as to give God a free hand to use us without consulting us. Let us accept whatever He gives and give whatever He takes with a big smile."

"All of us are but instruments who do our little bit and pass by."

"If it were not for God's tender love, every moment of the day, we would be nothing."

"If you are really humble, if you realize how small you are and how much you need God, then you cannot fail."

"When you talk about the Church — we all are the Church. We must not judge others, but ourselves." [14]

"In His Passion, Jesus taught us to forgive out of love, how to forget out of humility. So let us examine our hearts and see if there is any unforgiven hurt — and unforgotten bitterness." [15]

"Humility is strength."

"Humility is nothing but truth."

"There is a sort of miracle every day. There is not a day without some delicate attention of God, some sign of His love and care.... The greatest miracle is that God can work through nothings, small things like us. He uses us to do His work."

"You cannot learn humility from books; you learn it by accepting humiliations. Humiliations are not meant to torture us; they are gifts from God. These little humiliations —

if we accept them with joy — will help us to be holy, to have a meek and humble heart like Jesus." [16]

"Our life has all the more need of humility since it is so much in the public eye."

"As for me, I always say — the work is God's work. The poor are God's poor. I am just a little pencil in God's hand that He uses to send His message of love to the world."

"We must not drift away from the humble works.... It is never too small."

"Be faithful in little things, for in them our strength lies. To the good God, nothing is small. The moment we have given it to Him, it becomes infinite."

"Yes, my dear children, be faithful in little practices of love, in little fidelities which will build in you the life of holiness and make you Christ-like."

✠

From the *Constitutions of the Missionaries of Charity*:

We value silence as a necessary aid to prayer and as a sign of our sincere love and mutual concern for one another providing an atmosphere of peace and quiet in the community facilitating prayer, work, study, leisure, and rest. We will know how to discern in the light of love, how and when to speak, and when to keep silence.... We look forward to the profound silence as a holy and precious time, a withdrawal into the living silence of God.

Poverty

✠

"The poorer you are, the more Jesus will love you."

— St. Thérèse of Lisieux

Photo by Paul Hulewicz

As I sat at the bedside of a dying man in Calcutta, I found myself praying: "Dear God, give me the heart of the poor. Give me this humility, give me this goodness, this gentleness, meekness, purity, and holiness. Give me this spirit of simplicity and total surrender. Give me this complete trust in You."

Our Lord Jesus came into this world with nothing but love, and He left this world with nothing but love. His earthly life started in a simple wooden manger, and it ended on a simple wooden cross. He was covered with little other than a cloth at birth as well as at death, much like the poorest of the poor in India. Saint Bernard of Clairvaux pointed out that, "poverty was not found in heaven. It abounded on earth, but we did not know its value. Jesus, therefore, treasured it; and came down from heaven to choose it, to make it precious to us."

Saint Thérèse of Lisieux had been told that "the closer one approaches to God, the simpler one becomes." She said, "I understood that true greatness is to be found in the soul, not in a name. … It is in heaven, then, that we shall know our titles of nobility. Then shall every man have praise from God and the one who on earth wanted to be the poorest, the most forgotten out of love of Jesus, will be the first, the noblest, and the richest!"

Mother Teresa taught by her life and by her words, to "live simply. Give example through simplicity." She taught her own Missionaries of Charity sisters to embrace perfect poverty — to her, that meant having nothing but God. They would dress very humbly and simply, like the Blessed Mother of Christ. She said that "Jesus' way of poverty was simple: He trusted His Father completely." She wanted her Missionaries of Charity to grow in their spiritual life and to deepen their loving trust in God — to "become so united to God as to radiate Him." Mother often referred to the "freedom of poverty" — she believed that the less we have, the less we have to worry about. And if we do not have too many material things, then we will be more free to love God and to serve Him wholeheartedly and unreservedly. These words of Saint Thomas à Kempis always remind me of the Missionaries of Charity: "They were poor in earthly things, but very rich in grace and virtues."

Let us turn to more of Mother Teresa's words on poverty:

"The sisters are always smiling and happy. We are so free, we are so free. I think people are so preoccupied with material difficulties. In the industrial world where people are supposed to have so much, I find that many people, while dressed up, are really, really poor. By having nothing, we will be able to give everything — through the freedom of poverty." [17]

"God wants me to be a lonely nun, laden with the poverty of the cross. Today I learned a good lesson. The poverty of the poor is so hard. When I was going and going till my legs and arms were paining, I was thinking how they have to suffer to get food and shelter. Then the comfort of Loretto [her former convent] came to tempt me, but of my own free choice, my God, and out of love for You, I desire to remain and do whatever is Your holy will in my regard. Give me courage now, this moment."

— Excerpt from Mother Teresa's diary from her
early days as a Missionary of Charity [18]

"Many people don't understand why we don't have washing machines, why we don't have fans, why we don't go to cinemas, why we don't go to parties. These are natural things and there's nothing wrong in having them. But for us, we have chosen not to have."

— from the documentary film *Mother Teresa*,
by Ann and Jeanette Petrie

"Keep to the simple ways of poverty — of repairing your own shoes, and so forth — in short, of loving poverty as you love your mother." [19]

"Be clear as glass."

"There must be a reason why some people can afford to live well. But I tell you, this provokes avarice, and there comes the sin. Richness is given by God, and it is our duty to divide it with those less favored."

"The most terrible poverty is loneliness and the feeling of being unloved."

"Christ is in the poor and lonely. The certainty of this reality is boundless for me."

"Before God, we are all poor."

✠

Excerpted from a letter by Mother Teresa:

You have said "yes" to Jesus — and He has taken you at your word. The Word of God became man — poor; your word to God became Jesus — poor; and so this terrible emptiness you experience. God cannot fill what is full. He can only fill emptiness — deep poverty — and your "yes" is the beginning of being or becoming empty. It is not how much we really "have" to give — but how empty we are — so that we can receive fully in our life and let Him live His life in us. In you today, He wants to re-live His complete submission to His Father — allow Him to do so. Does not matter what you feel — that you have nothing — that you are nothing. Give Jesus a big smile — each time your nothingness frightens you. This is the poverty of Jesus. You and I must let Him live in us and through us in the world. Cling to Our Lady — for she too, before she could become full of grace, full of Jesus, had to go through that darkness. "How could this be done?" But the moment she said "yes," she had need to go in haste and give Jesus to John and his family. Keep giving Jesus to your people, not by words, but by your example — by your being in love with Jesus — by radiating His holiness and spreading His fragrance of love everywhere you go. Just keep the joy of Jesus as your strength. Be happy and at peace. Accept whatever He gives and give whatever He takes, with a big smile. You belong to Him. Tell Him, "I am Yours — and if you cut me to pieces, every single piece will be only all Yours." … Pray for me as I do for you.

Peace

✠

*"Let us go forward in peace, our eyes upon heaven,
the only goal of our labors."*

— St. Thérèse of Lisieux

*M*other Teresa was a token of God's love and peace to the world. I found these "Token of Love" stamps on the walls of the hotel where I was staying in Calcutta, and I learned that Mother's face appeared on *millions* of Indian postage stamps — "an unheard of honor for a nun and for someone born outside India."

Mother Teresa of Calcutta gave us all hope for justice and peace in a world full of injustice and chaos. No matter how bad things got in society, we could point to Mother and say that there was still hope for humanity! "Mother Teresa is among those emancipated souls who have transcended all barriers of race, religion, creed, and nation," stated the President of India, V. V. Giri, as he presented her with the prestigious Nehru Award in 1972. "In this troubled world of today, embittered by numerous conflicts and hatred, the life and work of Mother Teresa bring new hope for the future of mankind." This supernatural hope for peace radiated from her face and "lit up her words." More importantly, she *advanced* peace on earth by her reverence for life and by her extraordinary love. Malcolm Muggeridge wrote that Mother Teresa had given him "a whole new vision of what being a Christian means: of the amazing power of love, and how in one dedicated soul, it can burgeon to cover the *whole world*." [20]

Saint Thérèse of Lisieux once said: "With love, not only did I advance, I actually *flew*." I was in Calcutta with Mother Teresa and the Missionaries of Charity during the Persian Gulf War in early 1991. The United States State Department had issued a warning to all Americans not to travel to certain parts of the world, including India, and there were very few volunteers in Calcutta at this time. This made it a more intimate experience with Mother and the sisters.

Mother Teresa was speaking with two or three of us at her house one day while the war was still underway. She said something which I could never forget: "Let us fly over the Middle East, and look down, and pray for peace." I stood before her in silent amazement and I kept my eyes fixed on her. Solemnly and earnestly, she repeated: "Let us fly over the Middle East, and look down, and pray for peace." As extraordinary as these words were, I immediately understood them to mean that we should fly over the Middle East *in spirit*, like angels would do. Let us go there *spiritually* and look down over that troubled part of the world, and pray for peace. Love is not bound by time and space. Love is free to go where it pleases.

I knew that while Mother Teresa was encouraging us to embark on this peace mission, she herself was doing so. She was flying over the Middle East in spirit, looking down over that war-torn area, and praying for peace. Earnestly, and compassionately. I had never heard anyone say anything like this before. And yet it seemed so natural coming from the mouth of this living saint! It was so inviting and so beautiful to me, and I willingly joined her in this spiritual journey of love. Within two short days, the war abruptly ended. I will never forget it.

Today, while she is in heaven, I wish to invite her (and all the angels and saints!) to fly with us over the troubled areas of the world, and look down, and pray for peace. I think Mother is now in an even better place to make a more widespread difference in bringing peace to the world. The poorest of the poor knew Mother Teresa as the "angel of the slums." I know her as an angel of mercy for all of us, everywhere. She was an angel of peace, who sought to spread God's peace through works of love and the power of prayer.

Mother Teresa's words teach that when we begin to care for one another, there will be peace:

"Where there is love — there is peace, there is joy, there is unity."

"If we have no peace, it is because we have forgotten that we belong to each other."

"No matter how much evil there is in the world, Christ's love is always stronger."

"The greatest destroyer of peace today is abortion. Because it is a direct war, a direct killing."

"If we accept that a mother can kill even her own child, how can we tell people not to kill one another?"

"The child is God's gift to the family."

"Every single child is a child of God — created in the image of God."

"That unborn child has been carved in the hand of God."

"Instead of death and sorrow, let us bring peace and joy to the world."

"I have never been in a war before, but I have seen famine and death. I was asking myself what do they feel when they do this. I don't understand it. They are all children of God. Why do they do it? I don't understand." [21]

"We must live life beautifully; we have Jesus with us and He loves us. If we could only remember that God loves us, and we have an opportunity to love others as He loves us, not in big things, but in small things with great love, then [our country] becomes a nest of love … a burning light of peace in the world."

"If you only knew how I long to light the fire of love and peace throughout the world. Pray for me that He may use me to the fullest." [22]

"Let us not use bombs and guns to overcome the world. Let us use love and compassion."

"Works of love are always works of peace."

✠

Mother Teresa's words from *Architects of Peace: Visions of Hope in Words and Images*, by Michael Collopy:

The fruit of silence is prayer; the fruit of prayer is faith; the fruit of faith is love; the fruit of love is service; the fruit of service is peace.

Let us not use bombs and guns to overcome the world. Let us use love and compassion. Peace begins with a smile. Smile five times a day at someone you don't really want to smile at; do it for peace. Let us radiate the peace of God and so light His light and extinguish in the world and in the hearts of all men all hatred and love for power.

Today, if we have no peace, it is because we have forgotten that we belong to each other — that man, that woman, that child is my brother or my sister. If everyone could see the image of God in his neighbor, do you think we would still need tanks and generals?

Peace and war begin at home. If we truly want peace in the world, let us begin by loving one another in our own families. If we want to spread joy, we need for every family to have joy.

Today, nations put too much effort and money into defending their borders. They know very little about the poverty and the suffering that exist in the countries where those bordering on destitution live. If they would only defend these defenseless people with food, shelter, and clothing, I think the world would be a happier place.

The poor must know that we love them, that they are wanted. They themselves have nothing to give but love. We are concerned with how to get this message of love and compassion across. We are trying to bring peace to the world through our work. But the work is the gift of God.

Holiness

"All men, of every condition, in whatever honorable walk of life they may be, can and ought to imitate the most perfect example of holiness placed before men by God — namely, Christ Our Lord, and by God's grace arrive at the summit of perfection, as proved by the example of many of God's saints."

— PIUS XI,
IN HIS ENCYCLICAL ON CHRISTIAN MARRIAGE

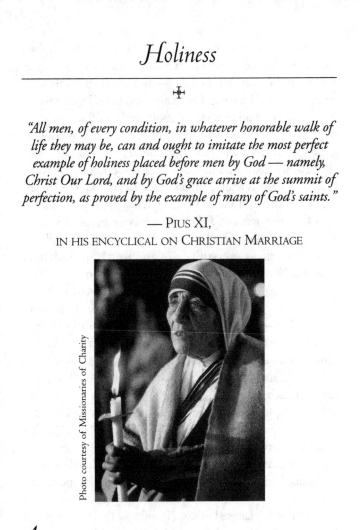

Photo courtesy of Missionaries of Charity

$\mathcal{A}$sk, and it will be given you; seek, and you will find" (Luke 11:9). Surprisingly, a big part of holiness consists in *receiving* — "receiving God from God," as Father Conrad De Meester would say — since God is holiness itself. Without receiving God's love and graces, His own Holy Spirit, we cannot be holy — no matter how much we do or give. So, let us come to Him often — and let Him fill us with every grace and blessing. Let us ask God to make us holy — to cleanse us of all that is not good, and to fill us with His own Spirit. "If you then, who are evil, know how to give good gifts to your children, how much more will the heavenly Father give the Holy Spirit to those who ask Him!" (Luke 11:13). As Mother Teresa used to say: "God is so delicately kind." And He is dying to make us holy.

Our Lord Jesus and the saints encourage us to look at nature. Flowers do very little — yet they fulfill His will and God gives them everything. In the words of Mahatma Gandhi: "A rose does not need to preach. It simply spreads its fragrance. The fragrance is its sermon." Little birds do very little — God gives them everything. Little children do very little — God gives them everything. And children tend to have more purity, love, and holiness than even the most remarkable and talented achievers in the world.

Children, with all their innocence, humility, love, and trust "preach without preaching — not by words but by their example;" and in the words of Our Savior Himself: "To such belongs the kingdom of God" (Luke 18:16). This is not to say that we should sit around doing little. It is simply to say that we should learn to trust God wholeheartedly and open ourselves to everything He wishes to pour out upon us.

Mother Teresa used to say, "If only we let Him do it, … He does it in a beautiful way." Let us allow Jesus to make us holy. Let us contemplate our Divine Master as He went about doing acts of mercy and spreading the Good News

— and in silent adoration, let us learn His own lessons of love and secrets of sanctity.

Let us now turn to the words of Blessed Mother Teresa of Calcutta:

" 'I will be a saint' means I will despoil myself of all that is not God."

"Holiness is not the luxury of the few — it is a simple duty for you and for me. We have been created for that. So let us be holy as Our Father in heaven is holy."

"Thoughtfulness is the beginning of great holiness. If you learn the art of being thoughtful, you will become more and more like Christ. His Heart was kind and gentle, and He always thought of the needs of others. Jesus did good wherever He went."

"If you are already a saint, thank God. If you are a sinner, don't remain one."

"Faithfulness to the inspirations of the Holy Spirit — that is the shortest route to holiness."
— St. Faustina Kowalska

"Thank God for the gift He has given you to show forth His beauty in this world. Let everything you do be done for the glory of God and the good of people."

"You have to be holy where you are — wherever God has put you."

"Our progress in holiness depends on God and on ourselves — on God's grace and on our will to be holy. We must have a real living determination to reach holiness. Let us ask Our Lady to help us to keep our hearts pure so that we can love Christ, her Son, with tenderness and love."

"Sanctity is a disposition of the heart which makes us humble and little in the arms of God – aware of our weakness and confident even unto audacity in the goodness of our heavenly Father."
— ST. THÉRÈSE OF LISIEUX

"We must become holy, not because we want to feel holy but because Christ must be able to live His life fully in us. We are to be all love, all faith, all purity.... And once we have learned to seek God and His will, our contacts with the poor will become the means of great sanctity to ourselves and to others." [23]

"True holiness consists in doing God's will with a smile."

"Faithfulness makes saints. The first step toward holiness is the will to become holy. Through a firm and upright will, we love God, we choose God, we hasten to God, we reach Him, we have Him." [24]

"Holiness does not consist in doing extraordinary things. It consists in accepting, with a smile, what Jesus sends us."

"Nothing can make us holy except the presence of God ... and to me the presence of God is in fidelity to little things."

"Make every effort to walk in the presence of God, to see God in everyone you meet."

> "If we trample our vices underfoot, we make of them a ladder."
>
> — St. Augustine

"God commands us to be holy, — and God cannot command the impossible."

"If we only let Him do it! We have only to let Jesus do it — and He does it in a beautiful way!"

"Jesus in us is our love, our strength, our joy, and our compassion."

"Am I convinced of Christ's love for me and mine for Him? This conviction is like a sunlight which makes the sap of life rise and the buds of sanctity bloom. This conviction is the rock on which sanctity is built." [25]

"Use the beautiful gifts God has given you for His greater glory. All that you have and all that you are and all that you can be and do."

"The greatest author of prayer is the Holy Spirit Himself. Jesus is our prayer and He is also the answer to all our prayers."

"Because of God's goodness and love, every moment of our life can be the beginning of great things."

"Holiness is union with God."

"Everyone can reach this love through meditation, spirit of prayer, and sacrifice, by an intense inner life."

"Give yourself fully to God. He will use you to accomplish great things on the condition that you believe much more in His Love than in your own weakness."

> "Great *love*, not great deeds, is the essence of sanctity."
> — St. Thérèse of Lisieux

"Jesus is going to do great things with you if you let Him do it and if you don't try to interfere with Him."

"Keep the light of Christ always burning in your heart."

"Often you see small and big wires, new and old, cheap and expensive electric cables up — they alone are useless and until the current passes through them, there will be no light. The wire is you and me. The current is God. We have the power to let the current pass through us and use us to produce the light of the world, or we can refuse to be used and allow the darkness to spread. My prayer is with each one of you and I pray that each one of you will be holy, and so spread God's love everywhere you go. Let His light of truth be in every person's life so that God can continue loving the world through you and me. Put your heart into being a bright light."[26]

"My heart is filled with joy and expectation of the beautiful things God will do through each one of you. Beautiful are the ways of God if we allow Him to use us as He wants."

"Jesus wants us to be holy as His Father is holy. We can become very great saints if we only want to. Holiness is not the luxury of the few, but a simple duty for you and for me."[27]

"Total surrender to God must come in small details just as it comes in big details. It's nothing but that single word, 'Yes, I accept whatever You give, and I give whatever You take.' And this is just a simple way for us to be holy. We must not create difficulties in our own minds. To be holy doesn't mean to do extraordinary things, to understand big things, but it is a simple acceptance, because I have given myself to God, because I belong to Him — my total surrender. He could put me here. He could put me there. He can use me. He cannot use me. It doesn't matter, because I belong so totally to Him that He can do just what He wants to do with me."[28]

"A day alone with Jesus is apt to spur us on in the vigorous pursuit of holiness through personal love for Jesus. Jesus desires our perfection with unspeakable ardor. 'For this is the will of God — your sanctification.' His Sacred Heart is filled with an insatiable longing to see us advance towards holiness."[29]

"One day Saint Margaret Mary asked Jesus: 'Lord, what wilt thou have me to do?' 'Give Me a free hand,' Jesus answered. He will perform the divine work of sanctity, not you, and He asks only for your docility. Let Him empty and amend you, and afterwards fill the chalice of your heart to the brim, that you in your turn may give of your abundance. See Him in the tabernacle; fix your eyes on Him who is the light; bring your hearts close to His divine Heart; ask Him to grant you the grace of knowing Him, the love of loving Him, the courage to serve Him. Seek Him fervently."[30]

Our Lady

✠

*"She is so beautiful that to see her again one
would be willing to die."*

— ST. BERNADETTE OF LOURDES

*O*h, what a beautiful Lady!" said young Blessed Jacinta,
with her hands clasping her face, after seeing Our Heavenly
Mother Mary in Fatima, Portugal, in May 1917.

Earlier, in the mid-1800's, Saint Bernadette could not
find adequate words to describe Our Lady as she appeared
to her in Lourdes, France: "Nothing here below comes close
to the beauty I have seen."

Mother Teresa referred to the Blessed Virgin Mary, the Mother of Christ, as "the most beautiful of all women, the greatest, the humblest, the most pure, the most holy.... A model for all women." She is "the spotless mirror of God's love."

Mother Teresa explained so simply that if there were no Mary, then there would be no Jesus — "no Mother, no Son."

One of Mother Teresa's great maxims was: "Be only all for Jesus through Mary." From the first summer that I met her, to the very last day of her life, she was telling us to "be only all for Jesus through Mary." She personally lived her devotion to Jesus and Mary so beautifully. She did everything *with* Our Holy Mother Mary, and she did everything *for* Our Lord Jesus, her Son.

In her last letter, dated September 5, 1997, Mother Teresa wrote: "I know that Mother says often, 'Be only all for Jesus through Mary,' but that is because that is all Mother wants for you, all Mother wants from you. If in your heart you are only all for Jesus through Mary, and if you do everything all for Jesus through Mary, you will be a true [Missionary of Charity]." You will be a true carrier of God's Love.

Mother Teresa's spiritual life revolved around Our Lord Jesus and Our Blessed Mother Mary — around Holy Eucharist and the Holy Rosary. "Let nothing and nobody ever separate you from the love of Jesus and Mary."

Mother Teresa particularly loved how Our Blessed Mother Mary cared for others — how she went in haste through the rugged hill country of Judea as soon as she found out that her cousin Elizabeth was expecting a baby in her old age. Not only was Our Lady practicing the sublime virtue of charity, but she was literally bringing the very real presence of Jesus with her — to bring great joy and peace to the one she served. As Mother Teresa said: "*Loving trust* and *total surrender* made Our Lady say 'yes' to the message of the angel, and *cheerfulness* made her run in haste to serve her cousin Elizabeth. That is so much our life — saying 'yes' to Jesus and running in haste to serve Him in the poorest of the poor. Let us keep very close to Our Lady and she will make that same spirit grow in each one of us" (emphasis added).

Let us turn again to Mother Teresa's words:

"God chose Mary because she was full of grace and yet so full of humility."

"We honor [Holy Mary] by praying the Rosary with love and devotion and by radiating her humility, kindness, and thoughtfulness towards others."

"The most wonderful part of redemption began in such a humble way. God did not send Gabriel to the palace of the great and rich, but to the young girl Mary in the one-room cottage at Nazareth. She asked but one question of the angel who announced she would be the mother of the Savior: 'How can this be?' And when he explained, she, being full of grace, offered herself as the handmaid of the Lord. This was why she was chosen — because although she was full of grace, she was also full of humility. She didn't think of the grace of the Son of God within her. She didn't dwell on the joy and sorrow that were hers as the Mother of God and of mankind. She only thought of how to serve, of how to fulfill her vocation as the handmaid of the Lord."[31]

> "Let Mary never be far from your lips and your heart. Following her, you will never lose your way."
>
> — ST. BERNARDINE OF SIENA

"Our Lady trusted God.... She said 'yes' continually with full trust and joy, trusting in Him without reserve."

"My gratitude is my fervent prayer for you that you may be humble like Mary so as to be holy like Jesus. Like Mary, let us be full of zeal to give Jesus to others. Like her, we too become full of grace each time we receive Jesus in Holy Communion."

"I am happy that you are well disposed and open to the will of God since that is of greatest importance in all we do. Cling to Mary and ask her to teach you how to love Jesus more and more since no one did the will of God as completely as she did."

"I ask Our Lady to give you her heart — so beautiful, so pure, so loving, so humble — that you may be so empty of self like she was and love Him as she loved Him and serve Him as she did, keeping close to Him even at the foot of the Cross."

"May Our Blessed Mother in her great love for you help you grow in her likeness through humility of heart and purity of life. She will see the needs of your heart too and will tell you to do whatever He tells you. So, continue to trust in her love for you."

> "Only after the Last Judgment will Mary get any rest; from now until then, she is much too busy with her children."
>
> — ST. JOHN VIANNEY

"Stand near Our Lady.... It is only with Our Lady that we can thank God properly."

"Nothing is impossible for those who call Mary their mother."

"Mother of God's little Child, I am little too. Take my hand and clear my path — lead me home to You. You're my Mother too. I depend on you. I am little like your little Child. / Mother of God's precious Child, I am precious too. Jesus came and died for me; He gave me to you. You're my Mother too. I belong to you. I am precious, like your precious Child. / Mother of God's holy Child, make me holy too. Keep my heart from every wrong, keep it close to you. You're my Mother too. I will trust in you. Make me holy, like your holy Child."

— MISSIONARIES OF CHARITY SONG

"Pray especially to Our Blessed Mother Mary, placing all your intentions into her hands. For she loves you as she loves her Son. She will guide you in all your relationships so that peace may fill your life."

"Our Lady knows us by heart and she will lead us to the surest and quickest path to holiness."[32]

"Let us entrust [our loved ones] to Our Lady's care. She will obtain for them the graces they need. She is our Mother indeed."

"Mary, Mother of Jesus, be a mother to me now!"

"Be with us, Mary, along the way. Guide every step we take. Lead us to Jesus, your loving Son. Come with us, Mary, come!"

— MISSIONARIES OF CHARITY SONG

"Keep very close to Our Lady."

"I am praying for you, asking Mary, Our Lady of the Way, to give you the light to know God's will for you, for the courage to accept it, and for the love to do it, cost what it may! Put your hand into the hand of Mary and ask her to help you."

Photo by Michael Collopy

"Mary, my Mother, give me your heart so beautiful, so pure, so Immaculate, so full of love and humility that I may be able to receive Jesus in the Bread of Life, love Him as you loved Him, and serve Hime in the distressing disguise of the poor."

"Learn from Our Lady who, when she saw Jesus humiliated and scourged, was not afraid to claim Him as her Son. Let us pray to her to fill our hearts with that trust, so that nothing and nobody will separate us from the love of Christ."[33]

Our Lord Jesus

✠

"Jesus, Jesus, Jesus."

— THE PRAYER ON MOTHER TERESA'S LIPS
DURING THE LAST MOMENTS OF HER LIFE

See! I will not forget you...
I have carved you
on the palm of My hand
I have called you
by your name.
You are mine.
You are precious to Me
I love you.

— Isaiah —

When Mother Teresa was barely 18 years old, she decided to become a missionary. Her mother knew that she had to let go of her young daughter forever — in fact, they were never able to see each other again. She gave her teenage daughter some simple advice that was forever engraved in her heart: "Put your hand in His — in His Hand — and walk all the way with Him."[34]

Mother Teresa's life was inseparable from her faith in Our Lord Jesus. Her entire mission of love for the poorest of the poor was built on the words that Jesus spoke to her personally, and the words He spoke to us all in Sacred Scripture. As she reached out to the most desperate and suffering souls, she would remind us of what Our Lord Jesus said: "For I was hungry and you gave me food, I was thirsty and you gave me drink, I was a stranger and you welcomed me, I was naked and you clothed me, I was sick and you visited me, I was in prison and you came to me.... Truly, I say to you, as you did it to one of the least of these my brethren, you did it to me" (Mt 25:35-36, 40).

Mother Teresa inspired us to satiate His thirst for love and for the salvation of souls by praying and also by reaching out to Him "in His distressing disguise of the poor." She wanted us to treat each emaciated dying person, each alcoholic, each orphaned child, each outcast of society with all the tenderness, love, and respect that we would give to Our Lord Jesus Himself. She wanted us to feed them as if we were feeding Christ Himself, and be with them in their suffering as if we were standing beneath the foot of the Cross. And she made His words easy to remember by taking my hand and pointing to each of my outstretched fingers and slowly enunciating each word that Jesus said: "*You did it to me.*" It was a lesson I could never forget. She was telling me to do unto others as I would do unto *Jesus Himself,* because in serving the "least" of humanity, I was directly serving God. Christ Himself said so.

Mother Teresa asked me to create a drawing of a little child in the palm of God's Hand. She wanted me to include the beautiful passage from the Old Testament in which God says to each one of us, through the prophet Isaiah:

"See! I will not forget you … I have carved you on the palm of My hand. I have called you by your name. You are mine. You are precious to Me. I love you." (see Isaiah 49:15-16). Mother knew that each human being was precious to God. She believed what He said. She would show this drawing to various individuals and tell them that the little child in God's Hand was that particular person — "This is how much God loves you; it is as if you are His only one." She would explain that He is protecting each one of us and guiding us. "God wants you, God loves you, God is with you, God cares for you."

Mother not only wanted us to know how much we were personally loved by God, but she also wanted so much for Our Savior to be loved in return as He deserves — tenderly, trustfully, fearlessly, and faithfully. She wanted so much for us to "love the Love that is not loved."

She taught us this simple prayer: "Jesus, I believe in Your tender, faithful love for me. I love You."

Let us turn to Mother Teresa's beautiful words about Our Lord Jesus:

"Pray for me, that I not loosen my grip on the hands of Jesus" [35]

"With Jesus, you can do all things."

"Without Jesus, our life would be meaningless, incomprehensible. Jesus explains our life." [36]

"All we do — our prayer, our work, our suffering — is for Jesus. Our life has no other reason or motivation…. I serve Jesus twenty-four hours a day. Whatever I do is for Him. And He gives me strength. I love Him…. He gives us the strength to carry on this life and to do so with happiness." [37]

"Jesus, come into my heart."

"In Holy Communion we have Christ under the appearance of bread. In our work we find Him under the appearance of flesh and blood. It is the same Jesus. 'I was hungry, I was naked, I was sick, I was homeless.'"

"Put yourself completely under the influence of Jesus, so that He may think His thoughts in your mind and do His work through your hands, for you will be all-powerful with Him who strengthens you."

"In my work, I belong to the whole world. But in my heart, I belong entirely to Christ."

"The good God wants just only our love and our trust in Him."

"God thirsts for you."

"Just think of Almighty God in the womb of Mary, locked in. He had to cling helplessly to His mother. This was the total surrender of Christ. Again, nailed to the cross, He could not move. Again today, He is bound in the tabernacle. This is total surrender."[38]

"I want to love Him with a deep personal love."

"He is the life that I want to live.
He is the light that I want to radiate.
He is the way to the Father.
He is the love with which I want to love.
He is the joy that I want to share.
He is the peace that I want to sow.
Jesus is everything to me.
Without Him, I can do nothing."[39]

"I want Him to be loved tenderly by many."

✠

Mother Teresa's Meditation (in the hospital, June 19, 1983):

"Who do you say I am?" (Matthew 16:15)

> You are God.
> You are God from God.
> You are begotten, not made.
> You are one in substance with the Father.
> You are the Son of the living God.
> You are the Second Person of the Blessed Trinity.
> You are one with the Father.
> You are in the Father from the beginning:
>   All things were made by You and the Father.
> You are the beloved Son in Whom the Father is well
>   pleased.
> You are the son of Mary,
> conceived by the Holy Spirit in the womb of Mary.
> You were born in Bethlehem.
> You were wrapped in swaddling clothes by Mary and
>   put in the manger full of straw.
> You were kept warm by the breath of the donkey
>   who carried your Mother with you in her womb.
> You are the son of Joseph, the carpenter as known by
>   the people of Nazareth.
> You are an ordinary man without much learning, as
>   judged by the learned people of Israel.

78

Who is Jesus to me?

Jesus is the Word made flesh.
Jesus is the Bread of Life.
Jesus is the victim offered for our sins on the Cross.
Jesus is the sacrifice offered at the Holy Mass for the
    sins of the world and mine.
Jesus is the word — to be spoken.
Jesus is the truth — to be told.
Jesus is the way — to be walked.
Jesus is the light — to be lit.
Jesus is the life — to be lived.
Jesus is the love — to be loved.
Jesus is the joy — to be shared.
Jesus is the sacrifice — to be offered.
Jesus is the peace — to be given.
Jesus is the Bread of Life — to be eaten.
Jesus is the hungry — to be fed.
Jesus is the thirsty — to be satiated.
Jesus is the naked — to be clothed.
Jesus is the homeless — to be taken in.
Jesus is the sick — to be healed.
Jesus is the lonely — to be loved.
Jesus is the unwanted — to be wanted.
Jesus is the leper — to wash his wounds.
Jesus is the beggar — to give him a smile.
Jesus is the drunkard — to listen to him.
Jesus is the mental — to protect him.
Jesus is the little one — to embrace him.
Jesus is the blind — to lead him.
Jesus is the dumb — to speak for him.
Jesus is the crippled — to walk with him.

Jesus is the drug addict — to befriend him.

Jesus is the prostitute — to remove from danger and befriend her.

Jesus is the prisoner — to be visited.

Jesus is the old — to be served.

To me — Jesus is my God.
  Jesus is my spouse.
  Jesus is my life.
  Jesus is my only love.
  Jesus is my all in all.
  Jesus is my everything.

Jesus I love with my whole heart, with my whole being.

I have given Him all, even my sins, and He has espoused me to Himself in tenderness and love.

Now and for life I am the spouse of my crucified Spouse.

Amen.

Holy Eucharist and Adoration

✠

*"I am the living bread which came down from heaven.
If any one eats of this bread, he will live for ever;
and the bread which I shall give for the life of the world
is my flesh."*

— OUR LORD JESUS CHRIST (JOHN 6:51)

We are taught that each of the sacraments of the Church is an encounter with God. Each sacrament brings us into the real presence of God. Especially since being with Mother Teresa, I realize that my greatest joy in life, my deepest peace and my favorite blessing is receiving Holy

Communion — the Most Blessed Sacrament. It never ceases to amaze me that we can be so *near* to our God as to actually receive Him and be filled with His own precious Body and Blood. Our good God allows us to partake of this "Bread of Angels" — this "Bread of Life and Cup of Eternal Salvation," and we are allowed to actually hold Him and carry Him as truly as His own Mother did. It is amazing that He desires so much to make His dwelling with us. It will take an *eternity* to thank Him properly for this most sublime privilege of being so close to Him as to be one with Him.

I have heard many people say that they wish they could have met Mother Teresa. Meeting Jesus is an even greater privilege, and Mother Teresa would be the first to say so. We have this incredible opportunity to personally visit with Christ every day. If souls really knew the truth about what takes place spiritually during Holy Communion, we would be crawling to Holy Mass each day. We would be going out of our way to have a "private audience" with Our Lord through receiving this inestimable treasure — this "Supreme Love-Gift: Jesus-the-Eucharist."

Mother Teresa began every day with Mass — with Holy Communion, because this "gives us the strength and the courage and the joy and the love to touch Him, to love Him, to serve Him. Without Him, we couldn't do it. With Him, we can do all things." She would say: "Our lives, to be fruitful, must be full of Christ."

In 1973, Mother Teresa and the Missionaries of Charity began having a Holy Hour of Adoration of the Blessed Sacrament *every day*. Prior to 1973, it had been a *weekly* Holy Hour. "From the time we started having Adoration every day," Mother said, "our love for Jesus has become more intimate, our love for each other more understanding, our love for the poor more compassionate."

Mother Teresa and her Missionaries of Charity considered these Holy Hours to be their "family prayer" when they "gather together to pray the Rosary before the exposed Blessed Sacrament the first half-hour, and the second half hour ... pray in silence."

Let us listen to Mother Teresa's words about the great gift of Jesus in the Most Holy Sacrament:

"Put your sins in the chalice for the Precious Blood to wash away. One drop is capable of washing away the sins of the world. The Eucharist is connected with the Passion. If Jesus had not established the Eucharist, we would have forgotten the crucifixion. It would have faded into the past and we would have forgotten that Jesus loved us. To make sure that we do not forget, Jesus gave us the Eucharist as a memorial of His love."

"Unless we have Jesus, we cannot give Him. That is why we need the Eucharist. It is true, our way of life is difficult. It has to be like that. It is not only the material poverty, but the poverty of being surrounded by suffering people, by death. Only the Eucharist, only Jesus, can give us the joy of doing the work with a smile."[40]

"To be able to bring His peace, joy, and love, we must have it ourselves, for we cannot give what we have not got."

"We become full of grace each time we receive Jesus in Holy Communion.... Let us thank God for all His graces."

"The beginning of Christianity is the giving. God so loved us that He gave His own Son. Jesus took bread, the simplest of

foods, and He made that bread into His Body. He made Himself the living Bread to satisfy our hunger for God."

"Jesus gave Himself totally."

"See how much Jesus loves us in the Blessed Sacrament."

"When you look at the Crucifix, you understand how much Jesus loved you. When you look at the Sacred Host, you understand how much Jesus loves you now."

"The Last Supper lasted about three hours. It was the Passion — Christ's love. That Bread was so expensive! Let us therefore eat this Bread. It is ours; Our Lord bought it for us and paid for it Himself. He gives it to us; we have but to take it."

— ST. PETER JULIAN EYMARD

"Jesus wants all of us to come to Him in the Blessed Sacrament. He is really there in person waiting just for you."[41]

"Nowhere on earth are you more welcomed, nowhere on earth are you more loved, than by Jesus living and truly present in the Most Blessed Sacrament. The time you spend with Jesus in the Blessed Sacrament is the best time that you will spend on earth. Each moment that you spend with Jesus will deepen your union with Him and make your soul everlastingly more glorious and beautiful in heaven, and will help bring about an everlasting peace on earth."[42]

"I will pray for you — that you do small things with great love, and become holy: only all for Jesus through Mary."

"How tenderly Jesus speaks when He gives Himself to His own in Holy Communion.... Oh, what could my Jesus do more than give me His Flesh for my food? No, not even God could do more nor show a greater love for me."[43]

"Holy Communion ... is the intimate union of Jesus and our soul and body. If we want to have life and have it more abundantly, we must live on the Flesh of Our Lord. The saints understood so well that they could spend hours in preparation and still more in thanksgiving. This needs no explanation, for who could explain 'the depth of the riches of the wisdom and knowledge of God'?"[44]

"Where will you get the joy of loving? — in the Eucharist, Holy Communion. Jesus has made Himself the Bread of Life to give us life. Night and day, He is there. If you really want to grow in love, come back to the Eucharist, come back to that adoration."[45]

"Every moment of prayer, especially before Our Lord in the tabernacle, is a sure positive gain. The time we spend in having our daily audience with God is the most precious part of the day."[46]

"When communicating with Christ in your heart after partaking of the Living Bread, remember what Our Lady must have felt when the Holy Spirit overpowered her, and she who was full of grace became full with the Body of Christ. The spirit in her was so strong that immediately she 'rose in haste' to go and serve."[47]

✠

Mother Teresa's letter to her Missionaries of Charity Sisters, Brothers, and Fathers, March 25, 1993:

My Dearest Children —

This letter … comes from Mother's heart. Jesus wants me to tell you again … how much love He has for each one of you — beyond all you can imagine. I worry some of you still have not really met Jesus — one to one — you and Jesus alone. We may spend time in chapel — but have you seen with the eyes of your soul how He looks at you with love? Do you really know the living Jesus — not from books, but from being with Him in your heart? Have you heard the loving words He speaks to you? Ask for the grace; He is longing to give it. Until you can hear Jesus in the silence of your own heart, you will not be able to hear Him saying, "I thirst," in the hearts of the poor. Never give up this daily intimate contact with Jesus as the *real living person* — not just the idea. How can we last even one day without hearing Jesus say, "I love you" — impossible. Our soul needs that as much as the body needs to breathe the air. If not, prayer is dead — meditation only thinking. Jesus wants you each to hear Him, speaking in the silence of your heart.

Be careful of all that can block that personal contact with the living Jesus. Devil may try to use the hurts of life, and sometimes our own mistakes, to make you feel it is impossible that Jesus really loves you, is really cleaving to you. This is danger for all of us. And so sad, because it is completely the opposite of what Jesus is really wanting, waiting to tell you. Not only that He loves you, but even more — He longs for you. He misses you when you don't come close. He thirsts for you. He loves you always, even when you don't feel worthy. When not accepted by others, even by yourself sometimes — He is the one who always accepts you. My children, you don't have to be different for Jesus to love you. Only believe — you are precious to Him. Bring all you are suffering to His feet — only open your heart to be loved by Him as you are. He will do the rest.

You all know in your mind that Jesus loves you — but in this letter Mother wants to touch your heart instead. Jesus wants to stir up our hearts, so not to lose our early love, especially in the future after Mother leaves you. That is why I ask you to read this letter before the Blessed Sacrament, the same place it was written, so Jesus Himself can speak to you, each one.

Why is Mother saying these things? After reading Holy Father's letter on "I thirst" [this refers to Pope John Paul II's homily on the "thirst of Jesus," which was printed in *L'Osservatore Romano* and which appears below], I was struck so much — I cannot tell you what I felt. His letter made me realize more than ever how beautiful is our vocation. How great is God's love for us in choosing our society to satiate that thirst of Jesus, for love, for souls — giving us our special place in the Church. At the same time we are reminding the world of His thirst, something that was being forgotten. I wrote Holy Father to thank him. Holy Father's letter is a sign for our whole society — to go more into this great thirst of Jesus for each one. It is also a sign for Mother that the time has come for me to speak openly of the gift God gave September 10 [the date, also known as "Inspiration Day," that Mother received her "call within a call" to leave everything and go out onto the streets of Calcutta to serve the "Poorest of the Poor" by founding the Missionaries of Charity] — to explain fully as I can what means for me the thirst of Jesus.

For me Jesus' thirst is something so *intimate* — so I have felt shy until now to speak to you of September 10 — I wanted to do as Our Lady who "kept all these things in her heart." That is why Mother hasn't spoken so much of "I thirst," especially outside. But still, Mother's letters and instructions always point to it — showing the means to satiate His thirst through prayer, intimacy with Jesus, living our vows — especially our 4th vow [wholehearted and free service to the poorest of the poor]. For me, it is so clear — everything in M.C. [the Missionaries of Charity] exists only to satiate Jesus. His words on the wall of every M.C. chapel, they are not from the past only, but alive here and now, spoken to you. Do you believe it? If so, you will hear, you will feel His presence. Let it become as intimate for each of you, just as for Mother — this is the greatest joy you could give me. Mother will try to help you understand — but Jesus Himself must be the one to say to you, "I thirst." Hear your own name. Not just once. Every day. If you listen with your heart, you will hear, you will understand.

Why does Jesus say "I thirst"? What does it mean? Something so hard to explain in words — if you remember anything from Mother's letter, remember this — "I thirst" is something *much deeper* than Jesus just saying, "I love you." Until you know deep inside that Jesus thirsts for you — you can't begin to know who He wants to be for you. Or who He wants you to be for Him.

The heart and soul of M.C. is only this — the thirst of Jesus' heart, hidden in the poor. This is the source of every part of M.C. life. It gives us our aim, our 4th vow, the spirit of our society. Satiating the living Jesus in our midst is the society's only purpose for existing. Can we each say the same for ourselves — that it is our only reason for living? Ask yourself — would it make any difference in my vocation, in my relation to Jesus, in my work, if Jesus' thirst were not longer our aim — no longer on the chapel wall? Would anything change in my life? Would I feel any loss? Ask yourself honestly, and let this be a test for each to see if His thirst is a reality, something alive — not just an idea.

"I thirst" and "You did it to Me" — remember always to connect the two, the means with the aim. What God has joined together let no one split apart. Do not underestimate our practical means — the work for the poor, no matter how small or humble — that make our life something beautiful for God. They are the most precious gifts of God to our society — Jesus' hidden presence so near, so able to touch. Without the work for the poor, the aim dies — Jesus' thirst is only words with no meaning, no answer. Uniting the two, our M.C. vocation will remain alive and real, what Our Lady asked.

... The thirst of Jesus *is* the focus of all that is M.C. The Church has confirmed it again and again — "Our charism is to satiate the thirst of Jesus for love and souls — by working at the salvation and sanctification of the poorest of the poor." Nothing different. Nothing else. Let us do all we can to protect this gift of God to our society.

Believe me, my dear children — pay close attention to what Mother is saying now — only the thirst of Jesus, hearing it, feeling it, answering it with all your heart, will keep the society alive after Mother leaves you. If this is your life, you will be all right. Even when Mother leaves you, Jesus' thirst will never leave you. Jesus thirsting in the poor you will have with you always.

That is why I want the active sisters and brothers, the contemplative sisters and brothers, and the fathers to each one aid the other in satiating Jesus with their own special gift — supporting, completing each other and this precious grace as one family, with one aim and purpose. Do not exclude coworkers and lay M.C.'s from this — this is their call as well; help them to know it.

Because the first duty of a priest is the ministry to preach, some years back I asked our fathers to begin speaking about "I thirst," to go more deeply into what God gave the society September 10. I feel Jesus wants this of them, also in the future — so pray Our Lady keeps them in this special part of their 4th vow. Our Lady will help all of us in this, since she was the first person to hear Jesus' cry, "I thirst," with Saint John, and, I am sure, Mary Magdalen. Because she was there on Calvary, she knows how real, how deep His longing for you and for the poor. Do we know? Do we feel as She? Ask her to teach — you and the whole society are hers. Her role is to bring you face-to-face, as John and Magdalen, with the love in the heart of Jesus crucified. Before it was Our Lady pleading with Mother, now it is Mother in her name pleading with you — "listen to Jesus' thirst." Let it be for each what Holy Father said in his letter — a word of life.

How do you approach the thirst of Jesus? Only one secret — the closer you come to Jesus, the better you will know His thirst. "Repent and believe," Jesus tells us. What are we to repent? Our indifference, our hardness of heart. What are we to believe? Jesus thirsts even now, in your heart and in the poor — He knows your weakness, He wants only our love, wants only the chance to love you. He is not bound by time. Whenever we come close to Him — we become partners of Our Lady, Saint John, Magdalen. Hear Him. Hear your own name. Make my joy and yours complete.

Let us pray.

God bless you,
M. Teresa, M.C.

Pope John Paul II's homily on the "thirst of Jesus" — preached on March 14, 1993, the third Sunday of Lent — which focuses on Christ's thirst for the gift of love from all whom the Father has given Him:

"Give me a drink" (John 4:7).

With these words, Jesus begins His lengthy, profound conversation with the Samaritan woman …

Tired from His journey, Jesus sits down at the well about noon. The natural thirst produced by the heat of that hour of day is the sign revealing *another thirst, a spiritual one*, which comes over His divine person: Jesus is thirsting for souls, seeking the faith and love which the Father has invited mankind to offer Him in full freedom by accepting Him as their Savior.

"Give me a drink!" Jesus asks the Samaritan woman not only for some water from a well dug many centuries earlier by the patriarch Jacob; He is asking her to acknowledge Him as the promised Messiah, the one who will give the living water of the Holy Spirit….

The dialog refers to another statement we find on Jesus' parched lips at the supreme hour of the Cross: "I thirst" (John 19:28). The image of the crucified *is the supreme sign of God's infinite love*.… One cannot remain indifferent to so great a love!

Dear brothers and sisters.… This is *the profound meaning of Jesus' thirst*.… The Son of God made man, who died to free us from sin, awaits the faithful and generous response of all whom the Father has given Him and who therefore belong to Him. He *thirsts for the gift of our love.*

As I stated in my recent Lenten message: "Today, Christ repeats His request and re-lives the torments of His Passion in the poorest of our brothers and sisters" (n. 1)....

You know well where to draw the light and strength for such a demanding mission...[from] a treasure that is the principal strength of evangelization: the Blessed Sacrament, source of all evangelization.

Your community, then, dedicated to the Blessed Sacrament, is called in a special way to give witness to respect and love for the sacrament of the Lord's Body and Blood. You will be helped and spurred on in doing this by your commitment to daily Eucharistic adoration....

May the program of adoration and prayer ... accompany you every day of the year. Gather up and present to the Lord the anxieties and sufferings, the toils and pains, the joys and hopes of everyone you meet on the way. May your whole life become a single offering to the Lord in union with the Redeemer's sacrifice....

I entrust your good intentions to the motherly protection of Mary, whom you venerate under the meaningful title of "Our Lady of Pardon." May she obtain from the Lord that forgiveness that is the sign of His infinite love and gives us in turn the strength to forgive and love our brothers and sisters.

... "Lord, you are truly the Savior of the world; give me the living water, that I may never thirst again."

— *L'OSSERVATORE ROMANO*, MARCH 17, 1993

"When we see her praying, we feel like praying!"
said one of the M.C. sisters, regarding Mother Teresa

$\mathcal{A}$t 4:40 a.m., a bell rings and the Missionaries of Charity arise for the day. One of the sisters calls out, "Let us bless the Lord!" The other sisters in the dormitory room reply, "Thanks be to God!" Then they recite prayers in the chapel, in the presence of Our Lord. Mother Teresa and the Missionaries of Charity always remove their sandals before entering the chapel, knowing that they are entering upon holy ground. That small gesture, in itself, is like a prayer. This little act of love and respect puts them in the right frame of mind when approaching our Heavenly Father.

Many of the following prayers are daily prayers from Mother Teresa's prayer book:

ACT OF FAITH

We firmly believe all the sacred truths the holy Catholic Church believes and teaches, because they have been revealed by You, the sovereign Truth, Who neither can deceive nor be deceived, and by the assistance of Your holy grace, we are resolved to live and die in the communion of this, Your Church.

ACT OF HOPE

Relying upon Your goodness, power, and promises, we hope to obtain pardon of all our sins and life everlasting, through the merits of Your Son Jesus Christ, our only Redeemer, and by the intercession of His Blessed Mother and all the saints. Amen.

ACT OF LOVE

We love You with our whole heart and soul, because You, O God, are most worthy of our love. We desire to love you as the blessed do in heaven. We adore all the designs of Your divine providence, resigning ourselves entirely to Your will. We also love our neighbor, for Your sake, as we love ourselves; we sincerely forgive all who have injured us, and ask pardon of all whom we have injured. Amen.

ACT OF DESIRE (*slightly adapted*)

May the burning and most sweet power of Your love, O Lord Jesus Christ, we implore You, absorb our minds, that we may die through love of You, Who were graciously pleased to die through love of us.

Immaculate Heart of Mary, cause of our joy, pray for us, bless us, help us to do all the good we can, keep us in your most pure Heart, so that we may please Jesus — through you, in you, and with you.

O God, we recommend to Your fatherly care the Pope, cardinals, bishops, priests, and all religious, all those who have asked for our prayers, and for whom we should pray.

BEFORE MEDITATION

O God, we firmly believe that we are in Your most holy presence, we believe that You see us — and that at this moment You behold even the inmost recesses of our hearts. Penetrated with this Your divine presence, we adore You, O God, with all the powers of our soul. We are unworthy to appear before You and more unworthy to hold communion with You. We are heartily sorry for having offended You and we beseech of You pardon of our sins and grace to make a good and fruitful meditation. We offer You all the thoughts of our minds, the affections of our hearts, and the operations of our souls. Imploring You to fill them with Your divine Spirit. Speak to us, O Lord, let us hear Your voice and attend to Your holy inspirations. Speak, Lord, for your servants are listening.

O Jesus! Grant that You may be the object of our thoughts and affections, the subject of our conversations, the end of our actions, the model of our life, our support in death, and our reward eternally in Your heavenly kingdom. Amen.

(Here, meditate on the sacred Scripture of the day, then conclude with the prayer, "After Meditation.")

AFTER MEDITATION

O holy Mother of God, throw your mantle of purity over our souls, and present us to your divine Son, Jesus, and give Jesus to us. Mary, our dearest Mother, we confidently turn to you. Holiest Mother, we beg you lend us your heart so beautiful, so pure, so immaculate, your heart so full of love and humility, that we may be able to receive and carry Jesus with the same sentiments with which you received and carried Him.

Come, O Mary, our queen and our mother, come and receive Jesus in us.

Take, O Lord, and receive all our liberty, our memory, our understanding, and our whole will, whatever we have and possess. You have given us all these; to You, O Lord, we restore them; all are Yours. Dispose of them in any way according to Your will. Give us Your love and Your grace, for this is enough for us. (From Saint Ignatius.)

PRAYERS AFTER COMMUNION

Radiating Christ

[Mother Teresa slightly adapted this beautiful prayer from one which was written by John Cardinal Newman. She prayed this every day after receiving Jesus Himself in Holy Communion. "I think if we can spread this prayer, if we can translate it into our lives, it will make all the difference," she said. "It is so full of Jesus."]

Dearest Jesus, help us to spread Your fragrance everywhere we go. Flood our souls with Your spirit and life. Penetrate and possess our whole being, so utterly, that our lives may only be a radiance of Yours. Shine through us, and be so in us, that every soul we come in contact with may feel Your presence in our soul. Let them look up and see no longer us, but only Jesus! Stay with us, and then we shall begin to shine as You shine; so to shine as to be a light to others; the light, O Jesus, will be all from You, none of it will be ours; it will be You, shining on others through us. Let us thus praise You in the way You love best — by shining on those around us. Let us preach You without preaching, not by words but by our example, by the catching

force, the sympathetic influence of what we do, and the evi-
dent fullness of the love our hearts bear to You. Amen.

+LDM

Missionaries of Charity,
54A, Lower Circular Rd.
Calcutta 700016.

7th March, 1987.

Dear Susan,

Thank you very much for your letter
and the prayer of St. Francis of
Assisi that you have sent.

It will be a beautiful thought if
you could share this prayer with
your circle of friends and it would
bring them peace and joy too.

Give the joy of loving through sharing.

God bless you
lee Teresa mc

Prayer for Peace
Lord, make me a channel of Your peace,
That where there is hatred, I may bring love;
Where there is wrong, I may bring the
    spirit of forgiveness;
Where there is discord, I may bring harmony;
Where there is error, I may bring truth;
Where there is doubt, I may bring faith;
Where there is despair, I may bring hope;

Where there are shadows, I may bring light;
Where there is sadness, I may bring joy;
Lord, grant that I may seek rather to comfort
than to be comforted;
To understand than to be understood;
To love than to be loved;
For it is by forgetting self that one finds,
It is by forgiving that one is forgiven,
And it is by dying that one awakens to eternal life.
Amen.

Anima Christi
Soul of Christ, sanctify me.
Body of Christ, save me.
Blood of Christ, inebriate me.
Water from the side of Christ, wash me.
Passion of Christ, strengthen me.
O Good Jesus, hear me.
Within Thy wounds, hide me.
Suffer me not to be separated from Thee.
From the malicious enemy, defend me.
In the hour of my death, call me
And bid me come unto Thee,
That with Thy saints, I may praise Thee
Forever and ever. Amen.

PRAYER OF POPE PAUL

Make us worthy, Lord, to serve our fellow men throughout
the world who live and die in poverty and hunger. Give
them, through our hands, this day their daily bread, and by
our understanding love, give peace and joy.

PRAYERS FOR OUR SOVEREIGN PONTIFF

Let us pray for our Sovereign Pontiff, Pope (*name*). May the Lord preserve him and give him life and make him blessed on earth and deliver him not to the will of his enemies.

Let us pray: O Almighty and Eternal God, have mercy on Your servant, Pope (*name*), our Sovereign Pontiff and direct him, according to Your clemency, in the way of everlasting salvation, that by Your grace he may desire such things as are agreeable to Your holy will and perform them with all his strength through Jesus Christ, our Lord. Amen.

PRAYER TO SAINT MICHAEL

O glorious Saint Michael the Archangel, prince of the hosts of heaven, who stands always for the help of the people of God, who did fight with the dragon, that old serpent, and cast him out of Heaven and valiantly defends the Church of God, we beg of thee from the bottom of our hearts to assist us in this difficult and dangerous combat which we, weak and infirm creatures, have to wage with the same enemy, that we may manfully resist and happily overcome him. Amen.

VENI CREATOR

(Prayed on Thursdays and Sundays.)

Creator Spirit all divine
Come visit every soul of Thine
And fill with Thy celestial flame
The hearts which Thou, Thyself didst frame.

O gift of God Thine is the sweet
Consoling name of Paraclete
And spring of life, and fire of love
And unction flowing from above.

The mystic sevenfold gifts are Thine,
Finger of God's right hand divine,
And Father's promise sent to teach
The tongue a rich and heavenly speech.

Kindle with fire brought from above
Each sense, and fill our hearts with love,
And grant our flesh so weak and frail
The strength of Thine which cannot fail.

Drive far away our deadly foe
And grant us Thy true peace to know,
So we, lead by Thy guidance still,
May safely pass through every ill.

To us through Thee the grace be shown
To know the Father and the Son
And Spirit of them both may we
Forever rest our faith in Thee.

To Father, Son be praises meet,
And to the Holy Paraclete,
And may Christ send us from above
That Holy Spirit's gift of love.

VENI CREATOR

(Prayed daily, *except* Thursdays and Sundays.)

Come Holy Spirit Creator blest
And in our souls take up Your rest,
Come with Your grace and heavenly aid
To fill the hearts which You have made.

To you the Comforter we cry
To You, the gift of God Most High,
The fount of life and fire of love
And souls anointing from above.

Make to us the Father known,
Teach us the eternal Son to own,
Be this our never changing creed
That You from them both proceed.

To God the Father let us sing,
To God the Son our risen King,
And equally let us adore
The Spirit God forever more.

V. Send forth Your Spirit and they shall be created.

R. And You shall renew the face of the earth.

Let us pray (in thanksgiving for our vocation, for our parents, and benefactors):

O God, You teach the hearts of the faithful by sending them the light of the Holy Spirit, grant us by the same Spirit to have a right judgment in all things and ever more to rejoice in His holy comfort. Amen.

MEMORARE

Remember, O most gracious Virgin Mary, that never was it known that anyone who fled to your protection, implored your help, or sought your intercession, was left unaided. Inspired with this confidence, we fly unto you, O Virgin of virgins, our mother; to you we come, before you we stand, sinful and sorrowful. O Mother of the Word Incarnate, despise not our petitions, but in your clemency hear and answer us. Amen.

SUNDAY PRAYER

Lord Jesus Christ, in the depths of Your Heart You adore the Eternal Father; from Him You come as radiant Son, begotten in the love of the Holy Spirit. Bring us close to Your Heart that we, too, sharing Your divine son-ship, may adore the Father Who created us in Your likeness. Heavenly Father, bring all those who do not know You to the creative love revealed in the Heart of Your Son. Amen.

MONDAY PRAYER

We praise and adore You, Divine Providence. We resign ourselves entirely to all Your just and holy designs.

Eternal God, Your eyes are upon all Your works, especially intent of Your servants. Turn away from us whatever is hurtful and grant us whatever is advantageous, that through Your favor and under the benign influence of Your special providence, we may securely pass through the transitory dangers and difficulties of this life, and happily arrive at the eternal joys of the next, through Christ our Lord. Amen.

TUESDAY PRAYER

Holy Angels, our advocates, *pray for us.*
Holy Angels, our brothers, …
Holy Angels, our counselors, …
Holy Angels, our defenders, …
Holy Angels, our enlighteners, …
Holy Angels, our friends, …
Holy Angels, our guides, …
Holy Angels, our helpers,…
Holy Angels, our intercessors, …
Lamb of God, You take away the sins of the world.
  Have mercy on us. (*3 times*)

Let us pray:
O Holy Angels, guardians of the poor confided to our care, we entreat your intercession for them and for ourselves. Obtain of God to crown His work by giving a blessing to our endeavors, that so we may promote His greater honor and glory procuring their salvation, through Christ our Lord. Amen.

WEDNESDAY PRAYER

O glorious Saint Joseph, we most humbly beg of you, by the love and care you had for Jesus and Mary, to take our affairs, spiritual and temporal, into your hands. Direct them to the greater glory of God, and obtain for us the grace to do His holy will. Amen.

THURSDAY PRAYER

Lord Jesus, Our God and Savior, we believe that You are present in this Sacrament of Your love, a memorial of Your death and resurrection, a sign of unity and a bond of charity. In Your humanity, You veiled Your glory. You disappear still more in the Eucharist, to be broken, to become the food of men. Lord Jesus, give us the faith and strength to die to ourselves in order to become a harvest for You so that You may continue, through us, to give life to men. May our minds be ever filled with You, the pledge of our future glory. Amen.

FRIDAY PRAYER

O Sacred Heart of Jesus, humbly prostrate before You, we come to renew our consecration, with the resolution of repairing, by an increase in love and fidelity to You, all the outrages unceasingly offered You. We firmly propose:

The more Your mysteries are blasphemed,
    The more firmly we shall believe them, O Sacred Heart of Jesus!

The more impiety endeavors to extinguish our hopes of immortality,
The more we shall trust in Your Heart, sole hope of mortals!

The more hearts resist Your divine attractions,
The more we shall love You, O infinitely amiable Heart of Jesus!

The more Your divinity is attacked,
The more we shall adore it, O divine Heart of Jesus!

The more Your holy laws are forgotten and transgressed,
The more we shall observe them, O most holy Heart of Jesus!

The more Your sacraments are despised and abandoned,
The more we shall receive them with love and respect, O most liberal Heart of Jesus!

The more Your adorable virtues are forgotten,
The more we shall endeavor to practice them, O Heart, model of every virtue!

The more the demon labors to destroy souls,
The more we shall be inflamed with a desire to save them, O Heart of Jesus, zealous lover of souls!

The more pride and sensuality tend to destroy abnegation and love of duty,
The more generous we shall be in overcoming ourselves, O Heart of Jesus!

O Sacred Heart, give us so strong and powerful a grace that we may be Your apostles in the midst of the world, and Your crown in a happy eternity. Amen.

SATURDAY PRAYER

O Heart of Mary, Heart of the tenderest of Mothers, cause of our joy, we consecrate ourselves unreservedly to you — our hearts, our bodies, our souls. We desire to belong to you, in life and in death. You know, O Immaculate Mother, that your Divine Son has chosen us in His infinite mercy in spite of our misery and sinfulness, not only as His children, … but also as His victims, to console His Divine Heart in the Sacrament of His love, to atone for sacrileges, and to obtain pardon for poor sinners. We come today, to offer Him through your most Pure Heart, the entire sacrifice of ourselves. Of our own free choice we renounce all the desires and inclinations of our corrupt nature; and we accept willingly and lovingly whatever sufferings He may be pleased to send us. But conscious of our weakness, we implore you, O holy Mother, to shield us with your maternal protection and to obtain from your Divine Son all the graces we need to persevere. Bless our society, this house, and the houses we visit, and each soul confided to our care; bless our relatives, friends, and benefactors, that all may persevere in grace or recover it if lost, and when the hour of death comes, may our hearts, modeled on your Immaculate Heart, breathe forth their last sigh into the Heart of your Divine Son. Amen.

PRAYER TO JESUS CRUCIFIED

Behold, O kind and most sweet Jesus, I cast myself upon my knees in Your sight, and with the most fervent desire of my soul I pray and beseech You that You impress upon my heart lively sentiments of faith, hope, and charity, with a true contrition for my sins and a firm purpose of amendment; whilst with deep affection and grief of soul I ponder within myself and mentally contemplate Your five wounds, having before my eyes the words which David the prophet put (on my lips) concerning You: "They have pierced my hands and my feet, they have numbered all my bones."

THE GREAT HEALER

[This beautiful prayer hung over one of the beds of the poor patients in the Home for the Dying in Calcutta. We would turn to our dear God every day to ask for all the grace, love, and courage we needed, and then we would turn to our dying brothers and sisters with our hands to serve.]

"Dearest Lord, the Great Healer, I kneel before You,
since every good and perfect gift must come from You.
I pray, give skill to my hands, clear vision to my mind,
kindness and sympathy to my heart.
Give me singleness of purpose,
strength to lift at least part of the burden of my suffering fellowmen,
and a true realization of the privilege that is mine.
Take from my heart all guile and worldliness,
that will the simple faith of a child I may rely on You."

PRAYER TO BE RECITED WITH
THE CRUCIFIX (*slightly adapted*)

O Jesus, by the wound in Your right hand (*kiss it*), give me a great love for the virtue of poverty, and grace to understand and live it faithfully.

O Jesus, by the wound in Your left hand (*kiss it*), give me a great love for the virtue of chastity — and grace to understand and live it faithfully.

O Jesus, by the wound of Your right foot (*kiss it*), give me a great love for the virtue of obedience — and grace to understand and live it faithfully.

O Jesus, by the wound of Your left foot (*kiss it*), give me a great love for the virtue of charity — and grace to understand and live it faithfully.

O Jesus, by the wound of Your sacred side (*kiss it*), give me the grace of perseverance in Your holy service, in this society, and a martyr's death. Amen.

"Martyrdom does not consist only in dying for one's faith. Martyrdom also consists in serving God with love and purity of heart every day of one's life."[48]

— St. Jerome

PRAYER TO THE HOLY SPIRIT

Breathe in me, O Holy Spirit — that my thoughts
  may all be holy.
Act in me, O Holy Spirit — that my work, too, may
  be holy.
Draw my heart, O Holy Spirit — that I love but what
  is holy.
Strengthen me, O Holy Spirit — to defend all that is
  holy.
Guard me then, O Holy Spirit — that I always may
  be holy.

DAILY PRAYER FOR ENLIGHTENMENT

Come, O blessed Spirit of Knowledge and Light,
and grant that I may perceive the will of the Father;
show me the nothingness of earthly things,
that I may realize their vanity
and use them only for Thy glory and my own salvation,
looking ever beyond them to Thee and Thy eternal
  rewards.

*M*any souls, many saints, have endured "the dark night of the soul" — periods when they no longer felt the sweet and comforting presence of God. These souls *willed* to believe in God, regardless of what they *felt*. They *willed* to love, and they *willed* to smile and to persevere in prayer, regardless of what they *felt*. Their faith and love were not based on emotions. Mother Teresa used to tell us that we must *will* to be holy. We must have a strong living *determination* to be holy. We must really want it and be firmly resolved to attain it, no matter how we *feel* on any given day.

Those who experience the "dark night of the soul" — the deep silence of God, "the feeling of not being loved by God," and the feeling that God does not even exist — are actually the best evangelizers, because they truly understand the experience of the vast majority of souls in this world. They can identify with the souls who are most in need of mercy.

We are just now beginning to learn about the interior darkness, loneliness, and struggles that Mother Teresa endured during her mission of love for the poorest of the poor. What anguish of heart she experienced after she began this ministry! It was the anguish of being alone, and even the anguish of feeling that God had abandoned her. It makes her warm *smile* and her spirit of *joy* that much more profound and inspiring when we realize that she was not swimming in interior consolations. It was not *easy* to smile — and yet she continued to do so.

"In my soul I feel just that terrible pain of loss, of God not wanting me, of God not being God, of God not really existing.... The darkness is so dark and the pain is so painful, but I accept whatever He gives and I give whatever He takes," Mother Teresa wrote. "With joy I accept all to the end of life."[49]

This new revelation about Mother Teresa's interior struggles makes her even more dear to us. We can relate to her much more deeply when we hear of her loneliness and weakness. And those revelations inspire us to persevere as she did in loving God even in the midst of trials, and smiling at others even when we are in pain, and keeping a rock-solid faith even at times when it seems like heaven does not exist.

A new book will be published revealing very intimate aspects of Mother Teresa's spirituality. I have been granted permission by Father Brian Kolodiejchuk, M.C., the Postulator for Mother Teresa's Cause for Canonization, to share a few of the precious gems that will later be revealed in full. Before Mother was called home to God, we did not realize that she had enjoyed such intimate and supernatural conversations with Our Lord, nor did we realize the "dark night of the soul" into which she was subsequently plunged, which lasted for approximately 50 years, until the end of her life. Only now are these hidden things being brought to light.

Long before she had even imagined founding a new religious order, when Mother Teresa was in her early thirties, she had expressed these beautiful sentiments towards Our Lord: "I have tried to live up to His desires. I have been burning with longing to love Him as He has never been loved before." Mother Teresa wanted "to give Jesus something very beautiful," "something without reserve" — and she solemnly vowed, in 1942, to "give God anything that He may ask — not to refuse Him anything."[50]

Our Lord took her at her word. He personally called her to go out among the very poor — "the sick, the dying, the little street children" — to radiate His love on those souls which were so precious to Him and so in need of mercy. It is amazing to imagine now that Mother felt this task was beyond her abilities, and she was afraid. She actually pleaded lovingly with Our Lord to find someone else who would be more worthy, more capable of such a mission! Jesus reminded Mother Teresa of her promise — "you have been always saying: 'do with me whatever You wish.' Now I want to act. Let me do it.... Do not fear. I shall be with you always.... Trust Me lovingly, trust Me blindly."

Mother privately shared with her confessor the details of what Our Lord Jesus had said to her with regard to her new mission of love to which He was calling her. These are the beautiful and poignant words of Jesus Himself: "My little one, come, come, carry Me into the holes of the poor.

Come, be My light. I cannot go alone. They don't know Me, so they don't want Me. You come, go amongst them. Carry Me with you into them. How I long to enter their holes, their dark, unhappy homes. Come … in your love for Me, they will see Me, know Me, want Me. Offer more sacrifices, smile more tenderly, pray more fervently, and all the difficulties will disappear. You are afraid; how your fear hurts Me. Fear not. It is I who am asking you to do this for Me. Fear not. Even if the whole world is against you, laughs at you, your companions and superiors look down on you, fear not. It is I in you, with you, for you. You will suffer, suffer very much, but remember I am with you. Even if the whole world rejects you, remember you are My own and I am yours only. Fear not, it is I. Only obey — obey very cheerfully and promptly and without any questions. Just only obey. I shall never leave you if you obey."[51]

Mother practiced such total surrender to God's Will. In an article titled: "The Soul of Mother Teresa: Hidden Aspects of Her Interior Life," Father Brian Kolodiejchuk wrote: "Mother Teresa experienced a real interior struggle between the love inspiring her determination to give God everything He was asking, and the fears and doubts arising from her sense of her own unworthiness and weakness. Yet … she was ready to 'burn herself completely' so that Jesus could be known and loved through her service to the poor."

Father Brian continued: "Mother Teresa also came to understand this trial as an opportunity to share the sufferings of Christ, Who took upon Himself the sins of the human race and offered Himself in sacrifice to the Father for the redemption of the world. Burdened with the iniquities of us all, He cried out from the Cross: 'My God, my God, why have You abandoned Me?'" Mother Teresa

Prayer for the Canonization of Blessed Teresa of Calcutta

✠

Photo courtesy of Missionaries of Charity

*J*esus, You made Mother Teresa an inspiring example of firm faith and burning charity, an extraordinary witness to the way of spiritual childhood, and a great and esteemed teacher of the value and dignity of every human life. Grant that she may be venerated and imitated as one of the Church's canonized saints.

Hear the requests of all those who seek her intercession, especially the petition I now implore … (*mention here the favor you wish to pray for*).

May we follow her example in heeding Your cry of thirst from the Cross and joyfully loving You in the distressing disguise of the poorest of the poor, especially those most unloved and unwanted.

We ask this in Your Name and through the intercession of Mary, Your mother and the mother of us all. Amen.

[With ecclesiastical approval. Please report any favors or miracles received through the intercession of Blessed Teresa of Calcutta to: The Postulator, 54A, A.J.C. Bose Road, Calcutta-700016, India]

Prayer to Blessed Teresa of Calcutta

✠

*B*lessed Teresa of Calcutta, longing to love Jesus as He had never been loved before, you gave yourself entirely to Him, refusing Him nothing. In union with the Immaculate Heart of Mary, you accepted His call to satiate His infinite thirst for love and souls and become a carrier of His love to the poorest of the poor. With loving trust and total surrender you fulfilled His will, witnessing to the joy of belonging totally to Him. You became so intimately united to Jesus your crucified Spouse that He deigned to share with you the agony of His Heart as He hung upon the Cross.

Blessed Teresa, you promised to continuously bring the light of love to those on earth; pray for us that we also may long to satiate the burning thirst of Jesus by loving Him ardently, sharing in His sufferings joyfully, and serving Him wholeheartedly in our brothers and sisters, especially those most unloved and unwanted. Amen.

[With ecclesiastical approval. Please report any favors or miracles received through the intercession of Blessed Teresa of Calcutta to: The Postulation of the Cause for the Canonization of Blessed Teresa, 54A, A.J.C. Bose Road, Kolkata-700016, India]

MISSIONARIES OF CHARITY
54/A A.J.C. Bose Road
Calcutta 700016 W.B.
INDIA

30th Apr. 2004

Dear Susan E. Conroy,

We have received your letter dated
on Mar. 14th 2004. Thank you for
all that you do to encourage people
to pray.

I am happy to hear all the good work
you are doing. Our Mother used to
say "the greatest author of prayer
is Holy Spirit Himself, Jesus is
our prayer and He is also the
answer to all our prayers".

Enclosed are some prayer cards and
a picture with Mother's favourite
inspirational sayings and a meditation which Mother herself wrote.

May the good Lord reward you for all
and all you do may help you to build
a close relationship with Jesus and
His Blessed Mother.

With prayers for you and for all the
good work you do.

God bless you,

M. Nirmala M.C.

Sr. M. Nirmala MC

Sources

For all the quotations by the Carmelite saints — Saint Thérèse of Lisieux, Saint John of the Cross, and Saint Teresa of Ávila — I refer you to ICS Publications in Washington, D.C.

Catholic Digest.

Cunningham, Frank, editor. *Words to Love By.* Based on interviews by Micahel Nabicht and Gaynell Cronin. Ave Maria Press, 1983.

Egan, Eileen. *Such a Vision of the Street.* Doubleday & Company, Inc. 1985.

Gonzales-Balado, Jose Luis, editor, and Janet N. Playfoot. *My Life for the Poor.* Harper & Row, 1985.

Hunt, Dorothy, editor. *Love: A Fruit Always in Season.* Ignatius Press, 1987.

Kolodiejchuk, Fr. Brian, M.C. "The Soul of Mother Teresa: Hidden Aspects of Her Interior Life."

Mother Teresa. *Jesus, The Word to Be Spoken.* (Quotations compiled by Angelo D. Scolozzi.) Servant Publications, 1986.

Mother Teresa. *The Love of Christ: Spiritual Counsels.* Harper & Row, 1992.

Mother Teresa. *Loving Jesus with the Heart of Mary,* by Fr. Martin Lucia, SS.CC.

Mother Teresa. *Thirsting for God.* (Quotations compiled by Angelo D. Scolozzi.) Servant Publications, 2000.

Muggeridge, Malcolm. *Something Beautiful for God.* Ballantine Books, 1971.

Spink, Kathryn. *Life in the Spirit: Reflections, Meditations, Prayers.* Harper & Row, 1983.

Endnotes

✠

[1] Eileen Egan. *Such a Vision of the Street*. Doubleday & Company, Inc. 1985

[2] Mother Teresa. *The Love of Christ: Spiritual Counsels*. Harper & Row, 1992

[3] Hunt, Dorothy, editor. *LOVE: A Fruit Always in Season*. Ignatius Press, 1987.

[4] Eileen Egan. *Such a Vision of the Street*. Doubleday & Company, Inc. 1985.

[5] Mother Teresa. *The Love of Christ: Spiritual Counsels*. Harper & Row, 1992.

[6] Cunningham, Frank, editor. *Words to Love By*. Based on interviews by Micahel Nabicht and Gaynell Cronin. Ave Maria Press, 1983.

[7] *Catholic Digest*, January 1994.

[8] Fr. Brian Kolodiejchuk, M.C. "The Soul of Mother Teresa: Hidden Aspects of Her Interior Life."

[9] *Catholic Digest*, April 1993.

[10] Mother Teresa. *Thirsting for God*. (Quotations compiled by Angelo D. Scolozzi.) Servant Publications, 2000.

[11] Eileen Egan. *Such a Vision of the Street*. Doubleday & Company, Inc. 1985.

[12] *Ibid.*

[13] *Ibid.*

[14] *Ibid.*

[15] *Ibid.*

[16] Mother Teresa. *Thirsting for God*. (Quotations compiled by Angelo D. Scolozzi.) Servant Publications, 2000.

[17] Cunningham, Frank, editor. *Words to Love By*. Based on interviews by Micahel Nabicht and Gaynell Cronin. Ave Maria Press, 1983.

[18] Eileen Egan. *Such a Vision of the Street*. Doubleday & Company, Inc. 1985.

[19] Mother Teresa. *The Love of Christ: Spiritual Counsels*. Harper & Row, 1992

[20] Eileen Egan. *Such a Vision of the Street*. Doubleday & Company, Inc. 1985.

[21] *Ibid.*

[22] *Ibid.*

[23] Malcolm Muggeridge. *Something Beautiful for God*. Ballantine Books, 1971.

[24] Mother Teresa. *The Love of Christ: Spiritual Counsels*. Harper & Row, 1992

[25] Eileen Egan. *Such a Vision of the Street*. Doubleday & Company, Inc. 1985.

[26] Spink, Kathryn. *Life in the Spirit: Reflections, Meditations, Prayers*. Harper & Row, 1983.

[27] Mother Teresa. *Jesus, The Word to Be Spoken*. (Quotations compiled by Angelo D. Scolozzi.) Servant Publications, 1986.

[28] *Ibid.*

[29] *Ibid.*

[30] *Ibid.*

[31] Mother Teresa. *Thirsting for God*. (Quotations compiled by Angelo D. Scolozzi.) Servant Publications, 2000.

[32] *Ibid.*

[33] *Ibid.*

[34] Eileen Egan. *Such a Vision of the Street*. Doubleday & Company, Inc. 1985.

[35] *Catholic Digest*. June, 1994.

[36] Gonzales-Balado, Jose Luis, editor, and Janet N. Playfoot. *My Life for the Poor*. Harper & Row, 1985.

[37] *Ibid.*

[38] Mother Teresa. *Thirsting for God*. (Quotations compiled by Angelo D. Scolozzi.) Servant Publications, 2000.

[39] Mother Teresa. Sung by Bradley James on the music CD titled: "Gift of Love."

[40] Eileen Egan. *Such a Vision of the Street*. Doubleday & Company, Inc. 1985.

[41] Letter by Mother Teresa. *Loving Jesus with the Heart of Mary*, by Fr. Martin Lucia, SS.CC.

[42] *Ibid.*

[43] Mother Teresa. *Jesus, The Word to Be Spoken*. (Quotations compiled by Angelo D. Scolozzi.) Servant Publications, 1986.

[44] *Ibid.*

[45] *Ibid.*

[46] *Ibid.*

[47] *Ibid.*

[48] *Catholic Digest*, July 1993

[49] Fr. Brian Kolodiejchuk, M.C. "The Soul of Mother Teresa: Hidden Aspects of Her Interior Life."

[50] *Ibid.*

[51] *Ibid.*

[52] Eileen Egan. *Such a Vision of the Street.* Doubleday & Company, Inc. 1985.

Praying in the Presence of Our Lord ...

Father Benedict J. Groeschel, C.F.R., internationally known lecturer
and retreat master is the author and/or series editor of
Praying in the Presence of Our Lord series.

Praying in the Presence of Our Lord: Prayers for Eucharistic Adoration
By Fr. Benedict J. Groeschel, C.F.R.
0-87973-586-4, (ID# 586) paper

Praying in the Presence of Our Lord with the Saints
By Fr. Benedict J. Groeschel, C.F.R., and James Monti
0-87973-948-7, (ID# 948) paper

Praying in the Presence of Our Lord with St. Thérèse of Lisieux
By Monica Dodds
1-59276-042-2, (ID# T93) paper

Praying in the Presence of Our Lord for the Holy Souls
By Susan Tassone
0-87973-921-5, (ID# 921) paper

Praying in the Presence of Our Lord for Children
By Fr. Antoine Thomas, f.j.
1-931709-95-5, (ID# T52) paper

Praying in the Presence of Our Lord with Fulton J. Sheen
By Michael Dubruiel
0-87973-715-8, (ID# 715) paper

Praying in the Presence of Our Lord with Dorothy Day
By David Scott
0-87973-909-6, (ID# 909) paper

Praying in the Presence of Our Lord with St. Thomas Aquinas
By Mike Aquilina
0-87973-958-4, (ID# 958) paper

In the Presence of Our Lord
By Father Benedict J. Groeschel, C.F.R., and James Monti
0-87973-920-7, (ID# 920) paper

Available at bookstores. Or, call Our Sunday Visitor
at 1-800-348-2440, ext. 3. Order online at www.osv.com.

OUR SUNDAY VISITOR
200 Noll Plaza, Huntington, IN 46750
For a free catalog, call 1-800-348-2440   A53BBBBP